Repression or Revolution?

REPRESSION OR REVOLUTION?
Therapy in the United States Today

*Michael Glenn
and Richard Kunnes*

HARPER COLOPHON BOOKS
Harper & Row, Publishers
New York, Evanston, San Francisco, London

Contents

A Note to Therapists

We don't want this book to be a mindless attack on therapists. They are not the "enemy." The enemy is the U.S. ruling class, which is bent on controlling the world for profit, and which uses therapy as one of its tools for controlling people. Therapists are caught in a contradiction: on the one hand, wanting to help people, and on the other, oppressing them for the system and making a living from people's suffering. Faced with this contradiction, most therapists choose to continue the oppression, persuaded that they have no other real choice. Therapy institutions are rigid and controlling, not meaningful and flexible. That is why so many well-intentioned therapists wind up doing piggish things.

Many therapists earnestly wish they could help people: in a new therapy commune, in a youth program, in a program aimed at helping kids before they begin to get messed up, in a community-run program, and so forth. Many innovative techniques and many well-meaning programs are born from these wishes, but wind up smashed by the facts of therapy as an institution in the United States. Creative people find out there's nowhere to go for funds. Innovative people learn that jobs are vulnerable. Efforts meant to help people seem to upset people's supervisors. Faced with this, many therapists settle for second best. They choose some degree of autonomy in a piggish system. Not oppressed themselves—although they complain of feeling alienated and of doing meaningless work—still they oppress others: diagnose them, fill out papers on them, hospitalize them against their will, medicate them, push conventional clichés at them. Therapists, like many people, feel powerless to change the system in which they function because they are detached from the working masses. They will not risk "deprofessionalizing" themselves, identifying their interests with the clients' rather than the bosses'. Thus they do the dirty work for the system a bit more glamorously than wardens, a bit less dangerously than cops, but dirty work all the same. In spite of all their hopes for "bringing about social change through individual and institutional reform," they wind up bolstering the system which gives them their bread. If they don't enforce this system, they get fired.

When the chips are down, most therapists have shown that their main identification is with the system, with their privilege. That doesn't mean they're not nice people who love their kids and hate war. But it does mean they accept being used by the system to oppress and control masses of working and poor people.

That's what this book is about—how therapy and therapists are used in this country. It's an illusion that therapy is value free; an illusion that being a therapist means you're automatically a helper of people. Help may come, but that's almost always secondary. Primary is the oppression which comes down on people all the time, and which therapy and therapists often embody and rarely decrease.

Although we sympathize with therapists' personal dilemmas, we identify with the struggles of people around the world for liberation. We see these struggles as primary, and the therapist's own personal situation as a secondary factor with which the therapist alone must deal.

Preface

We should clarify one aspect of this book. Although published in 1973, it was conceived in 1970–1971. Through writing and rewriting it, we have seen our ideas develop as objective conditions in the United States have changed. The "new left" of the 1960s has given way to new movements; being part of these we find ourselves somewhat critical of our former ideas. For example, we are much more aware of class issues today than we were a few years back. We understand these changes dialectically though—our current positions have evolved from our past ones—and we understand the importance of the "radical therapy" movement of the past few years. This book, then, reflects a certain historical time.

Readers will pick up various inconsistencies and changes in the book. Hopefully they will serve to clarify radical therapy as it evolved between 1970 and 1973. In some places we've tried to focus more on the politics we're now following; in others we've tried to make a clear statement of an earlier position. At any rate, we feel this book represents a process. We hope it raises questions for therapists, clients, and lay people. We hope it makes people wonder what the role of any "therapy" under capitalism can be. We hope it helps therapists and others reflect on how their programs serve the people and how they oppress them.

There is a fundamental contradiction in many human-service jobs. People's needs—for food, medical care, counseling, communication—may be served, but in the process the ruling class is further enhanced and entrenched. Such jobs are created to oppress people, to perpetuate the system by channeling needs through bourgeois institutions, and to inculcate bourgeois values. Most human-service workers want to serve others, not just aggrandize themselves. But objectively they realize that the service aspect of their work is often secondary to its social-channeling function. How this contradiction is resolved will determine the kind of human services and the kind of society this country will achieve.

Repression or Revolution?

Introduction

In today's rapidly changing world, therapy[1] serves the status quo. It bolsters the power of those who run the country. Therapy distorts reality, and then presents this distortion as the Truth Unveiled, which it presses on people, exhorting them to accept it and *adjust* to what they cannot change. When people insist that their own perceptions are true and that therapy is wrong—when, for instance, they point to mental hospitals as agencies of institutional oppression, to the brutalization of women in most marriages, to treatment of children as property, to schools which typically function as discipline factories—therapy answers by denying such perceptions. If that fails, therapy appeals to its experts for authoritative statements, or pronounces a diagnostic curse on its opponents, calling them "sick" or "maladjusted," in an attempt to discredit and neutralize them. Therapy also insists that the "real" problems are found (1) inside people's heads/emotions, (2) in the context of the family, or (3) in the breakdown of personal relationships. At each point, social and political realities are passed over, and the "blame" for emotional problems is laid on the people themselves.

[1]Throughout the book we have used the word "therapy" to encompass all forms of treatment—i.e., psychology, psychiatry, psychoanalysis, psychotherapy, and so on.

We don't deny individual responsibility, and we understand the importance of these factors. But in this book we will try to show how therapy and other social/political institutions serve to make people crazy and bludgeon them emotionally, even while trying to help. Therapy has confused people about their lives and encouraged them to retreat into their own "sick" selves and relationships rather than to deal with their overall living situation. In this book we will show how this has happened, and toward what end.

The trailblazing iconoclasm of early psychoanalysis has ebbed: Therapy is big business now, a part of the American way of life. The therapist's role is to maintain our society's conventional values and institutions, and thus to bolster the system which gives co^2 such status. Though it tries to wrap itself in the images of Philippe Pinel (who unchained the inmates of Paris's La Salpêtrière in 1803) and Sigmund Freud (who first explored the dark areas of the unconscious), therapy today is neither liberating nor revolutionary. Instead, it enslaves people, polices, diagnoses, drugs, and institutionalizes them. It is a political tool wielded by those with power. The professed "neutral" or "objective" aim of its practitioners is no more than rhetoric. In our oppressive society, therapy serves the oppressors.

Several books written in the past few years attack psychiatry or therapy from a liberal position.[3] They point out

[2]When the person's sex is unknown, we use the term "co" instead of the usual "he" and "him" and "cos" instead of "his" in this book as a way of ending sexism in our language.

[3]Shulamith Firestone, *The Dialectic of Sex* (New York: Morrow, 1970); Michel Foucault, *Madness and Civilization* (New York: Pantheon, 1965); Thomas S. Szasz, *Ideology and Insanity* (New York: Doubleday, 1970), as well as his many other books written in the past ten years; Erving Goffman, *Asylums* (New York: Doubleday, 1961); David Cooper, *Psychiatry and Anti-*

2

that treatment is not value free, that therapy programs are class biased, that drugs and therapy are used to blunt a patient's protest, that therapy has become allied with repressive forces in the society. We agree with this critique, but maintain that it doesn't go far enough: It still implies that with a few changes by benevolent professionals, therapy will be relevant and good and liberating once again. This is not true.

Therapy, no matter how benevolent and enlightened, still serves the interests of the ruling class. Some individuals may be helpful as therapists, but the overall impact of therapy systems and institutions remains unchanged. Unless therapy itself is totally changed in the light of a social revolution, nothing will be different.

Therapy is, in fact, one of the largest growth industries in the United States. Almost 2 million people a year flock to out-patient clinics; over 1 million a year enter mental hospitals, occupying half the country's hospital beds; another one-half million are in private therapy; larger numbers visit psychologically oriented clergymen, welfare workers, and teachers. Such a system is costly: about $4 billion a year, and almost 75 percent of it for outdated hospital services.

The federal government has pumped millions and millions of dollars into community mental health centers. Drug companies make millions a year from psychiatric drugs—antipsychotics, antidepressants, tranquilizers of a dozen varieties. Fired by the notion of "mental illness," newer services are being developed—day care and outreach clinics, for instance. But they bring the same old soup in new mugs. Mental health costs, fed by construction fees, salaries, and drug/hospital costs, continue to rise. The government has begun to reduce grants for training therapy professionals and for research—one of

Psychiatry (New York: Pantheon, 1971); Seymour Halleck, _The Politics of Therapy_ (New York: Science House, 1971).

the effects of the drain of the Vietnam War on our economy. The therapy community is perhaps beginning to understand the workings of a military/capitalist state, to realize that the war machine claims priority over human services. Its response, however, is to trail after the newest fad in grant money—whether for drug use, violence, suicide, or community control—rather than to try to work without the government's dominance/support. Once again, we see where therapy stands—right with the ruling interests.

Therapy exerts a profound influence on everyone. It affects the way we raise our children, envisage love, marry, educate people, experience sex, view ourselves, and distinguish crazy from normal. Therapists are the priests and gurus and faith healers of our time, the experts whose words we accept as truth.

Yet a person in emotional distress has a tough time getting help. People with money can buy care, although they rarely know their therapist's qualifications. Since anyone can call coself an analyst, therapist, psychoanalyst, psychotherapist, or counselor, the public is kept in the dark about what it's being promised. People without money have to rely on clinics, which are essentially cooling-out camps, or on state hospitals. Facilities for the treatment of common problems like drug addiction, alcoholism, acute crises, or family conflicts are few and overcrowded. Therapists prefer to offer what's convenient for themselves—long-term care for the wealthy, drug treatment and advice for the masses, hospitalization (where therapists-in-training do most of the work) for the suicidal, violent, or in any other way "problem" patient.

Treatment, wherever you can find it, puts patients one down. They come to the therapist feeling unhappy and upset: Something has happened to make them afraid or depressed, and they want help. Often a spouse, parent, court, or school has insisted on their seeking "professional help," implying that they're crazy and need a change in values and behavior. Often these third-party sources of payment will finance treatment *only* if the therapist calls the patient "mentally ill." Thus patients are fitted into an out-of-date and distorting medical model from the very beginning.

The system is cruel and oppressive, and therapists do little to change it. After all, they benefit from it. Almost all therapists are seen as "professionals" and enjoy vast privilege and considerable power. They are empowered by society to commit people to mental hospitals, to judge people's sanity and legal rights, to define "normal" and "abnormal," "healthy" and "sick." They are allowed to assault people with electroshock treatments, mind-numbing drugs, and other kinds of "therapy" that seek to remake or remold personalities. They bolster traditional myths about men and women, families, homosexuality, correct behavior, crime, and so on, by grinding out data used to support the ideology of the status quo. Educators and teachers pass on their "knowledge" to a new generation of establishment types, eager young people whose idealism soon gives way to cynical self-interest as they too perceive the power at their disposal.

The public, sold the virtues of therapy by the media, has been thoroughly mystified about what it really is.[4] People feel uninformed, dumb, foolish, crazy, unexpert— totally unable to decide for themselves what's right and what's wrong about therapy. They go to therapists for months or years, and sense that something's wrong with it. Yet they are afraid to confront the "expert," afraid to trust their own feelings because they are mystified and feel helpless and impotent. They try to play by the thera-

[4]This is an important concept for us. It refers to simple concepts which have been muddied over with professional-sounding jargon until they seem very complicated and difficult indeed, frightening people away from them. Of course, only "experts" can deal with things which have been mystified.

pists' rules, even though they'd really like to pursue their own goals. A radical, responsible therapy would meet *people's* needs, not the therapists'.

Therapy today comes from several sources:

1. The nineteenth century saw the rise of a medically controlled view of mental "illness," the growth of a system of state mental hospitals in the United States and of great asylums abroad, and the assumption of power by the "classic" diagnosticians and codifiers of mental illness. This tradition persists in American state hospitals and community clinics and in the majority of the diagnostic terms we use.

2. The development of psychoanalysis led to an "academic" tradition, cataclysmic and primitive in its imagery, which was threatening to the old myths and stereotypes of "human nature." Over the past two or three generations this vision has been dulled, turned over to clerks and bureaucrats, made into a series of dogmas and metaphysical abstractions with almost no relationship to the world of experience. Today it is influential in private practice, in the popular concept of therapy as "analysis," and in much of the current theory and training practices.

3. In recent years there has been a move toward "community" therapy. In practice, these are therapy programs for community people set up by those in authority, never by the community. (This phenomenon will be discussed later.)

Few therapists have as yet talked or written about society or oppression. Almost all of them (and almost all of them men) have elaborated theories of what goes on inside people's heads or, recently, of what goes on between people in a family or group. Except for Wilhelm Reich, parts of Alfred Adler, and Sigmund Freud's often reactionary, pessimistic views on society, almost no theorist has addressed coself to the interrelationship of individual and society. Around 1945, some of the neo-Freudians did begin to describe this area, but the discussion never acquired much strength in therapy circles, which remained individual-oriented. People who talked politics or social reality have been discouraged from therapy circles. Therapists are straight today, even those who wear "funky" clothes, speak hip language, or smoke marijuana in their pipes. They're not challenging the way things are at the roots, they're not committed to social change.

Every part of a social organism mirrors the whole. Therapy in an America marked by imperialism abroad, racism and sexism at home, antiyouth attitudes among elders, and oppression of the working class, takes on similar qualities. A society that denies people their feelings and perceptions from an early age, that encourages game playing and pretense, that concerns itself with power and consumption, and that treats people as things, very easily accepts the war in Vietnam, the slow genocide in the ghettos, the hippy-groovy individualism of the encounter-group scene and other therapy systems, and the scuffle for prestige and status. A country that devotes napalm and antipersonnel weapons to the large-scale slaughter of people in Southeast Asia must certainly drive many of its own people mad. But that "madness" is defined as "sanity": In a dehumanized world those who are still human become misfits, rejects, radicals, and "crazy." That's the awareness from which we begin this book.

People who have been driven crazy by the system, who have been oppressed so often that their human potential has been destroyed or narrowed down to a one-dimensional stereotype, are the ones who become "patients." People who are battered into confusion and despair become "psychotic." People who fear the destruction around them, who become aware of the inhuman, death-machine-like thrust of society become "paranoid." Current therapy is on the wrong side of the fence.

Of course, some people become psychotic in order, finally, to express lucid insights; but many others arrive there hopelessly confused and frightened, bludgeoned by the society around them. Our point of view, rather than romanticizing madness (as R. D. Laing sometimes does), sees it as wasted human suffering which wrecks people and keeps them from using their energy to transform society. Yes, sometimes madness is poetic, creative, fascinating; but more often it is painful. And the number of people not driven to dramatic madness, but only to bitterness, despair, irritability, and confusion, is incalculable in this country. Those are the 80 percent who need therapy according to the studies.

Then, of course, after contributing to the madness, our society provides "treatment" for it. This consists of further oppression: electroshock, enervating drugs, brainwashing disguised as talking-therapy, advice from "experts," internment, isolation, conditioning and deconditioning, behavior modification. As Claude Steiner has observed, "paranoia is a state of heightened awareness. Most people are persecuted beyond their wildest delusions."[5]

Part of the mystification about therapy is that it is a "medical" act. Thomas Szasz and others have shown this to be a myth. It is not something medical, or a branch of medicine, or part of the social sciences. Therapy is an essentially human activity which has been preempted and monopolized by a therapy elite and sold as a commodity on the open market.

The medical metaphor hides what therapy really is. Its language is confusing and hard to follow; its theory ob-

[5]Claude Steiner, "Radical Psychiatry Manifesto," *The Radical Therapist* (New York: Ballantine, 1971), p. 282.

scure. All the mystery makes it seem very complicated, indeed—an activity far beyond most of our understandings. Therapy can then go on, unchallenged, sticking people into asylums, experimenting with their bodies, serving all the while those in power. Patients become "patients" instead of people; therapists become "therapists" instead of people. The power differences in society are strengthened, not challenged or overturned. People have not demanded that their therapists be accountable to them; they have let therapists be privileged professionals, not workers. Therapists, many of whom are kind, sincere people, have been given a social position that cannot but turn them into oppressors.

We cannot forgive what's happened. People have been cruelly treated in the name of therapy. Therapy techniques read like a series of tortures from Dr. Caligari's chamber: lobotomy, water-dunking, electroshock, chemicals, whirling machines, chains, strait jackets. Women, blacks, Chicanos, young people, gays, poor people, dissidents, radicals, American Indians have all suffered at the hands of the therapy establishment.

It would be too simple to say that all therapists are pigs. Some are totally oppressive; others manage to be helpful at times, even though their place in society makes their goals hard to realize. Our point is that therapy is a piggish institution, corrupt and corrupting.

The main question is, what has therapy to offer? Therapy as it now exists opposes any real movement for social change; it helps a few individuals but obstructs many others. Therapists have not yet managed in any way to deprofessionalize themselves, to merge their interests with those of the working masses in this country. Innovations have brought new techniques and prestige to therapists, but few new programs are genuinely open to nonprofessionals and other community people.

We see this country moving toward revolution: a transfer of power from the few who rule now, to the masses.

Over the next decades the effects of worldwide U.S. imperialism will be coming home to roost. The economy will suffer more and more as other nations become communist and take a larger share of the world economic pie.

The U.S. working class, able until recently to live well compared to workers in the rest of the world, is finding its relative advantage slipping. Gains from imperialism have allowed the ruling class to buy off some workers while maintaining its own high profits. This process will slow down, unemployment will rise, and wages will lag behind inflation. Tensions in this country will increase, and the conditions for revolution will improve.

The world is changing, and we must either change with it or be left behind. What, eventually, will therapy be in this country? Whom will it serve? Will it be part of the movement for liberation and revolution? Or will it keep the ruling-class orientation which has marked it all these years? The answer seems evident: Therapy is part of the oppressive system, and therapists, by their acts, define themselves as antithetical to the people's interests. Therapy remains embedded in middle-class values and serves to maintain the class distinctions which exist today.

In the context of an advancing revolutionary struggle, therapy—as every other institution—must change. Therapy skills must be shared with the people and its institutions liberated, and given over to community control. Therapists must surrender their elite status and see themselves as workers, like other working people (doctors, carpenters, bus drivers, and so forth) who have useful skills. This book is meant to hasten this process, to help those without power to take it, to help those with therapy power to turn it over to the people.

Therapy can no longer be tolerated. It must be exposed and totally changed.

1

The State of Therapy Today

Therapy can't be separated from the way therapists live. It's important to know how the experts are handling their own lives and to understand their place in the political order.

The father of American psychiatry, Benjamin Rush, a signer of the Declaration of Independence and a famous medical humanist, stuck his son in an asylum at the age of twenty-one; he never came out. Is this a symbol of what's happened to American psychiatry?

Therapists today are a comfortable group. Psychiatrists make luxurious incomes—averaging $35,000 a year—and get a great deal of prestige and status along the way. Other therapists are catching up fast. Clinical psychologists and social workers, attracted to the newer encounter and group modes of therapy, are entering private practice by the dozens. And posts in new mental health centers are well-paid—in some parts of the country they are even going begging for lack of interested, qualified people. There's little radical thrust in therapy today simply because it is so profitable. Reformist efforts come from people near the bottom of the social heap—young people, women, therapists in less prestigious fields—not from professional therapists. The revolutionary push is coming from mental patients' liberation groups and from political collectives.

Therapists are sleek, well fed, and well dressed; they desire the status symbols of our society and are unwilling to take risks with their enormous affluence and power. After all, they have joined the respectable elements of society, the "pillars," the powerful, the elite. In some parts of this country, the chic "liberal" or "radical" therapist is tolerated, even encouraged to perform—to be a bit of a rebel, of course oppose the war, wear the season's hip clothes, kill one another when meeting or parting, regardless of sex. But the leash is slackened, not lengthened significantly. There are limits beyond which few venture lest they lose their status.

Almost one-third of all therapists work full time for third parties—that is, for schools, for the federal government (the Department of Defense, the National Institute of Mental Health), for prisons, for universities, for industry, for the police. Many more are part-time consultants who share their insights (and influence) with the ruling (oppressive) institutions. Their role is often to root out and stigmatize dissent or deviance, to help smooth over tensions so work can proceed unruffled, to maintain the existing order and help make it more efficient. They wield a terrible weapon: they can rubberstamp a person "sick."

Therapists in private practice also serve the status quo, but perhaps more subtly. Confined by an introspective, individualist-oriented view of people, they rarely involve themselves in challenging the social/political world and concentrate, instead, on helping people deal with their own heads. They try to come off as "neutral" when what they are, in fact, is "neutralizing." Rather than use therapy to strengthen people for a collective struggle which could change the real world, they are content to help people feel better, adjust to their lives, become more efficient, more arrogant, more competitive, more able to fight for themselves and grab a piece of the action. Groups encourage interaction but rarely reach political action together. The goals of private therapy are money for the therapist and "getting better" for the client. The treatment is supposed to function beyond morality and beyond politics. Such a situation makes therapy a reactionary force. For all their emphasis on personal liberation, therapists help people change only so far as the rest of society tolerates it. They rarely challenge the shared myths which helped drive the client crazy, or which created the tensions that drove co to seek treatment.

Thus therapists help people adjust to the conditions of their oppression, not change these conditions. The affluent are served in private practice; the disadvantaged are policed in community mental health programs. They cool people out and get them focused on their own heads and feelings from whence they never return. And the clients even foot this part of the bill for their continuing oppression. Indeed, they are supposed to be grateful too.

Many therapists are not even aware of this; they don't see their own bias. They've worked their whole lives with people of their own middle-class background. They're used to bright, verbal people, who receive "talking" therapy; they're also used to the dull, stolid, long-suffering people it's their duty to serve and profit from, whose therapy consists of drugs and hospitalization. Therapy, as a way of helping, works best (i.e., fulfills the patients' and therapists' goals) when client and therapist share the same orientation—class background, life values, meanings, culture. Middle-class white therapists seem to satisfy best the need of middle-class white patients—sometimes. The gap between the social position of most therapists and that of working class, dissident, or other groups (i.e., women) has become clearer lately, as our society becomes more and more clearly divided between the oppressed and the oppressors (even the oppressors today are bewailing how "oppressive" it is to be an oppressor). As awareness widens and deepens, popular suspicion of just what therapy is all about will increase.

The mystification of therapy today derives partly from its many varieties. There are psychoanalysts and plain analysts, psychiatrists, psychologists, social workers, occupational therapists, recreational therapists, reality therapists, primal scream therapists, encounter groupers, sensitivity people, body people, Freudians, non-Freudians, neo-Freudians, Jungians, Adlerians, drug experts, marathon experts, Gestaltists, brief therapists, nontherapists who insist that they are therapists, and so on. Anyone worth cos salt can hang out a sign and "do" therapy. The public, tormented and uncertain, in need of some kind of healing, goes where it's told to go. It's a seller's market, and the buyers are working in the dark. When they say that they can't see, they're met with arrogance. Why should they even expect to see? Certainly not before "treatment" is over.

Let's cut through some of this mystery and describe who therapists are. Among "professionally trained" people, there is a well-defined pecking order; those mentioned first have more training, more money, more prestige.

Psychoanalysts are usually M.D.s who have taken further residency training in psychiatry (up to three or four years) and who have completed additional training at an approved psychoanalytic institute (another five or so years, including a personal "training" analysis). These people, while not earning more money than anyone else —groupers and screamers, for instance, usually make much more, into the hundreds of thousands of dollars— have the highest academic prestige, and they represent an ideologically conservative element in the profession. The analysts with M.D.s are at the top of the heap and whether a school will admit non-M.D.s as psychoanalytic candidates is a matter of long-standing dispute. Psychoanalysts have been the researchers and teachers for the therapy profession, especially those who are medically oriented. They carry a sense of tradition with them. Though their prestige is falling now, their number still claims many bright, capable, insightful people. Concentrated in urban areas, the suburbs, and teaching centers, they tend to be politically liberal.

Psychiatrists are M.D.s who have completed three or more years of residency training in psychiatry. Many have been influenced by "organic" ideas of mental illness. Psychiatrists can prescribe drugs, and many rely strongly on them. They may have a job at the top of a mental health center. They see people once or twice a week or less (unlike analysts who may see people up to five times a week). Their education is usually very weak in the social sciences and humanities, as well as in simple psychological theory. Buttressed by their M.D. degrees, though, psychiatrists across the country tend to act as if they knew it all. They use drugs, electroshock, hospitalization, talking therapy, and any other technique they can think of. There's little evidence that much of what they do is effective, in spite of the media hard-sell, and the insurance companies' refusal to pay for non-M.D. treatment. They tend to be quite conservative, male, white, middle class, with a serious investment in the status quo.

Clinical psychologists have Ph.D. degrees in clinical, educational, or social psychology. They may be counselors at an institution, although lately growing numbers are entering private practice. Recently, many psychologists have become excited by group work and behavior-modification techniques. The former has attracted some radical, humanistic types and goes well with a flair for the spontaneous, a concern for personal growth, and an expressive personality. The latter is a copy of the medical/expert model where the psychologist manipulates cos clients with an assortment of techniques whose ineffectiveness seems fairly well established. The techniques tend to be used in a political vacuum, though, which is pretty scary. Groups of young, dissident psychologists have been forming lately, and the profession is under pressure to change its outlook. It remains to be seen how effective this will be.

Social workers have A.B. degrees and often some graduate training. They used to be limited to family visits but are now moving into other areas of experience: family and individual counseling, group work, institutional work. The effect of the women's liberation movement on the many women in this field has been profound. Because they experience firsthand the male chauvinism of those in power, the difficulty of being heard and listened to, the difficulty of affecting their places of work, they are a potentially very radical group. Their jobs, though, are usually at institutions, and so they are vulnerable to being fired, if they are too uppity and demanding, and having no job at all. This risk surrounding their job security affects not only them but the whole growing number of therapists in institutional work. It's as if they were first willing dupes of the system, but are now beginning to be locked in it as an insurance against their growing awareness of their piggish roles and the conflict of their behavior with their liberal ideals. Working for institutions makes it harder for anyone to oppose the institutions' power structure, and makes co vulnerable where it counts—in day-to-day survival. In addition, jobs are getting harder to find.

Social welfare workers, usually with only a B.A. degree, are physically close to people on welfare and often are forced to carry out the work of a brutal and dehumanizing system. They too form a potentially radical group and often have a choice between representing their clients' interests and challenging the system, or carrying out the system's brutality and maintaining their own jobs. Again, the ideals of these workers are often totally at odds with the actuality of their work. For these people, as for social

16

workers, jobs are getting harder to find; and as jobs get scarce (as they are in 1973), they will become less willing tools of the system.

Occupational therapists, mostly women, have had some professional schooling. Their work is primarily in the areas of job/skill training, in creative media, and more recently, in group and encounter work and sensitivity training. The spread of therapy work from the M.D.s and Ph.D.s to the other disciplines is an important step in ending the monopolization of therapy. All too often, however, the "paraprofessionals" proclaim themselves "professionals" and oppose the further spread of therapy skills just as the M.D.s and Ph.D.s did before them. That is, rather than encourage further demystification and sharing, they rush to join the therapy "in" group.

Recreational therapists, usually women with some special training, work mainly in institutions, as do most paraprofessionals. They focus on encouraging expression through artistic media—dance, clay, music, painting, woodwork—in the hope of helping patients get to their inner feelings. They also encourage group interaction and mutual problem solving. The recent tendency has been for RTs to do more innovative work, although their training encourages them to be traditional, subservient to the doctor's primary therapy goals, and somewhat intrapsychic in their interpretation of patients' activities and behavior.

Psychiatric nurses are trained to follow the medical model of emotional distress and almost all work for a hospital or clinic. They have been trained also to be women who follow men's orders. The women's movement, however, has inspired some to become vocal opponents of the sexism of current therapy and hospital work. Their jobs, like those of the social workers, are often in jeopardy as their awareness moves them more and more to confrontation with the authorities. One of their potential power bases is in the community they serve, especially when they themselves are community members of the same class background as their patients. They are a poorly-paid, often harshly exploited group of professionals.

Psychiatric aides and attendants who often have no college education at all, are on the bottom rung, socially and professionally. A few places like New York State have provided access to more highly skilled jobs for ambitious attendants, but most offer little chance of advancement. Attendants and aides are almost always of the same class as the clients they serve. They are employed in the hospital systems, both private and state, paid a ridiculously low wage, and pressured not to unionize. In spite of their low wages, they do the bulk of therapy work on the wards, as well as all the scut work. Of all hospital workers, they spend the most time with the patients. Many are women; many are black, Puerto Rican, Chicano, and poor. They have little effective power in most hospitals, unless they do group therapy. The organization of hospital workers is a vast, promising movement which would hopefully include not just attendants, but psychiatrists, cooks, elevator operators, laundry people, and so on—the entire "team" which makes hospital treatment possible. This is a focus for future struggle.

Professional nontherapists include group leaders, sensitivity trainers, people interested in self-realization and self-growth. They work at places like Esalen, and they believe that they provide growth or learning experiences. Though they agree their work often has a "therapeutic" function, they will not call it therapy. In spite of their rhetoric, however, their work is done under the guise of being "therapeutic" and "helping people get in touch with themselves." As such, it's still very much a part of the therapy establishment—and a rip-off. Many of the nontherapists come from nonmedical disciplines like education and the humanities and reject immediately any medical model of neurosis. They are more inclined to

18

see their work as teaching or providing new stimuli—the encounter-group people, for example, have developed many powerful, fascinating techniques for reaching into people's feelings. Some have even begun to open up the ways our bodies feel and the ways our memories and feelings are locked up in our muscle tensions and posture. Unfortunately, many have ignored the social/political milieu in which they work. Sometimes their focus on the individual has been crass and exploitative; and they have used their aura in groups for selfish power trips and sexual license. Emphasizing the freedom to "do your own thing," they appeal to today's youth cult. Yet their attitudes toward social issues tend to be reactionary. Still, their creative force is impressive, and it could be progressive. The future will tell on which side they finally ally.

Peer-counselors, although not formally therapists, work to help one another. They often have a highly formulated set of beliefs, trained group leaders, and a specific way of approaching their therapy function. Included here, for instance, are Alcoholics Anonymous, HELP, Schizophrenics Anonymous, Recovery, Inc., Self-Help, Reality House. They often treat groups of people called "untreatable" by others. Their politics are usually traditional and conservative.

In terms of strength of peer-group support, we should perhaps mention women's liberation groups (consciousness-raising groups), men's groups, and gay groups. Though some of their work is therapeutic—that is, helpful—they do not look upon themselves as therapy groups. They are organized more like a task-oriented consciousness-raising group with the potential to help support any of its members.

Finally, there is a whole array of "wild" therapists, people with little or no training or experience. Some are good; some atrocious. There's usually no way for anyone to find out in advance. These are the people who advertise in the underground media, offer services fairly cheaply, and emphasize "outsight" innovative techniques.

It's striking how many professionals cling to being a professional. They may fight among themselves, but they close ranks when therapy is under attack. Most therapists are united in their idea of "treatment" for the mentally ill or emotionally disturbed—a continuation of mystification and oppression. The professionals, accountable only to themselves, have served only themselves.

Professional organizations are, of course, controlled by the most conservative, most backward elements. They are obsessed with maintaining the professional standards and ethics. If they ever must change, they will change "slowly and deliberately." Recent groups pushing for change within the professions have been offered some recognition and support, and have tended to be sucked into the organization with a token position and with an increase in prestige and income. It's hard to pull away from professionalism's nuggets.

HOW IS THERAPY OPPRESSIVE?

Many therapists insist that they're not really oppressive, that therapy as an institution is liberating, that people who talk about external factors are often "projecting" and not facing up to their own "inner selves." Therapy, as we see it, is one way the ruling class controls the rest of the country: regulating people's lives without their consent, interfering, manipulating, brainwashing, institutionalizing, denigrating, neutralizing. That's what oppression is: controlling other people's lives and insisting on keeping that power, exploiting others to serve oneself and one's class, keeping others helpless and dependent. The entire structure of therapy supports this oppressiveness, from the one-up, one-down authoritarian (mystified) model to the myth of mental illness. Therapists have the power to put people away, to use drugs to control deviant and unwanted behavior, to keep women "in their place" and to call gay people "sick," to reinforce the family and its values, to see problems as personal rather than political. Therapy, moreover, is available only to those with money, the poor must go to low-cost, low-quality clinics. Therapy has, indeed, become a commodity, a means of social control, and as such, is no longer liberating. Even the personal-growth centers foster a crippling and selfish individualism, a greedy hedonism, and an elitist, enjoy-today view of the world. And all this occurs in a country filled with lonely, unhappy, anxious, depressed, angry, tense, oppressed, helpless, frustrated people. The treatment, unfortunately, has become part of the illness. It's our society itself, our America, that creates the tensions driving us crazy and alienating us from ourselves and one another. That's why treatment, in any radical sense, must change this society.

How did therapy systems get this way? Briefly, they developed like any other industry in a capitalistic society, like any other business built around product, consumer, seller, and profit. The myth of mental illness, particularly in recent years, was established, packaged, and sold. Just when the avant-garde in therapy was beginning to challenge and abandon the medical model, society swallowed it in toto. Professionals came to the front, started guilds and training groups, and began selling treatment to the public, advertising it through the mass media. The public, uncertain and uneasy, bought and is still buying. One of our teachers once said, "Mental health is the biggest growth industry in the country." He was right.

2

How Therapists Get the Way They Are and What Can Be Done about It

Walk into any mental hospital, clinic, or private office. Look around. The therapists' faces will be serious, tired, depressed, and businesslike; the dress sober. They have *work* to do, and they are serious about it. Their obsessional traits, lack of spontaneity, depressive mood, and overall straight characteristics are typical of most professionals in this country. Since they are responsible for dispensing therapy in this society, we need to understand how they are chosen and trained, how they develop their values, how they choose to act.

The making of therapists is one example of education turning well-intentioned people into oppressors. Candidates are preselected on the basis of personality type (obsessional) and social class (middle class, upward striving). Class values are maintained and professional values (ethics, standards) introduced that make therapists even more reactionary. They are forced to base their survival on the status quo: If they want jobs, they must perform "responsibly"—that is, in accordance with the traditions of their field. This makes it virtually impossible for them to affect their own future until they've been extensively exposed to the elite and its way of doing business. So long as therapy exists in its present institutionalized forms—training guilds, professional programs, myths of professional ethics and expertise, commercialism—therapists won't be different. It's questionable now whether therapists as a group even have that potential.

Therapists tend to be middle class, clever, verbal, manipulative people who have worked hard to get where they are; they've learned to do well at school, to compete successfully with peers. They are individualists who have made it, who sacrificed a good deal of present pleasure for future hopes and ambition. This affects them once they at last have the ability to satisfy their money/power/sex ambitions. Usually obsessional people—male, white, fairly well-to-do—and therapists come to believe strongly in the value of being a professional.[1] When they enter training, they continue along predictable lines. Few challenge them other than their supervisors and teachers (who usually are more conservative than they) whose task is to shape them.

Once in training, therapists live in a close-guild system, apprentices to masters. They are steeped in the myths of hierarchy and status as obvious values and are taught new manipulative techniques and "professional" skills, which will enable them to one-up patients. They are given a special identity, dependent on their practicing the craft like their elders. Imitation then becomes the clue to gaining status and prestige.

This makes them constantly vulnerable to conflict with authority. They learn to behave passively toward their superiors, and to disagree cleverly or politely, if at all.

[1]By obsessional character type, we mean people who are performance oriented, competitive and striving, individualistic; who want to be respected and famous rather than warm, loved, and loving (if there is a choice); who are more concerned with avoiding pain (humiliation, shame, guilt, anxiety) than with finding pleasure (love, fun); who are tight rather than loose; who take few risks.

They learn to be cautious, to think of themselves as naïve, inexperienced, and dumb. They bide their time, and unless they stupidly rock the boat, they'll be superstar-therapists too, someday, just like their hero-supervisors and teachers. This attitude toward authority, present in almost every professional field, helps explain the professionals' need to keep other people down—it's built into their character structure, and it's an integral part of the structure of our authoritarian/individualistic/competitive society.

Although many trainees have humanistic feelings, training blunts their awareness of others as people. Medical school discourages identification with the patient, discusses pathology rather than people, and teaches medical students to see a person as a problem—an obsessive, a marital problem, a situational disorder—just as a physician views kidney cases, or a lawyer sees malpractice suits. Training dehumanizes the trainee so that co can function better. It develops new cogs for old machines.

Most therapists in training are treated like fools. They are viewed as ignorant, clumsy, and naïve, incapable of valid perceptions, and racked by their own hang-ups. This may be the only time in their lives that they're genuinely treated like second-class (oppressed) people. But rather than see this (and remember it) and develop kinship with more oppressed people, they usually blind themselves to it, grit their teeth for the few more years of apprenticeship, and make plans for the future. Their transition from second-class trainees to middle-class professionals is easy and quick. In fact, they have always been part of the establishment. This brief oppressive experience is a necessary stage in their move toward greater things. Other oppressed people have little chance of getting out from under it, but the trainees' exit is clear, and they can well afford to be unaware of their place in the whole system.

When they challenge their supervisors' expertise, they

usually are treated like patients (sometimes, like fools) in need of therapy themselves. They grow to expect this tactic and to use it on their clients (and friends). They become always guarded, always one-up, always inviolate and invulnerable, safe and protected in their elite world of power. As trainees, their insights were squashed and they were made to feel inadequate; as therapists they will cover this feeling over by adopting rigid, prefabricated ideas and self-serving behavior with clients, and by mystifying the fact that they are ignorant and only pretending to be very, very wise indeed.

For all their training, therapists are usually themselves mystified about therapy and about what their role as therapists is. Since few people actually tell them what to do or provide direct supervision, and since almost all therapists have their own way of doing things, the young therapist *feels* co knows almost nothing about what co is doing. Inadequacy, confusion, and the sense that everyone else knows more affect every young therapist we've ever met, and make them all sitting ducks for their supervisors.

One acquaintance, for example, was told by a supervisor not to be so "active" because it was a sign of countertransference and overidentification with the patient; instead, he should have been quieter, more impersonal. Rather than comply with this, he continued to be active but reported none of his behavior to his supervisor. The supervisor was satisfied.

Another therapist gave some of her clothes to an adolescent patient whose parents refused to buy her any as a form of punishment; the therapist was severely reprimanded for "acting out." The patient, of course, experienced the act as warm and human, and was confused at the furor it caused the therapist.

Another therapist took a shy, young male patient for a walk. Outside the formal office setting, the two developed a much more open, more human interchange about their feelings. The therapist's supervisor was concerned, insist-

ing that this might be an "acting out," which would inter-
fere with the therapy.

Similarly, two young therapists questioned the sense of
an in-patient group in which the therapists remained passive and relied on the patients' spontaneity for cues—the
results had been close-lipped patients and long silences.
They were told *not* to be active and that they were simply anxious and unfamiliar with group techniques. When
they began to innovate and become more active and less
"professional" anyway—and, in fact, to achieve results—
they were told that this was simply a way of challenging
their supervisors' authority.

We could go on forever. When therapists do things
their supervisors disagree with, the supervisors imply
that the therapists are sick. Very few ever discuss the
issues face-to-face.

One supervisor, in meeting with the patient council,
constantly challenged and shot down patients' suggestions; he then berated the patients for not taking more
responsibility for themselves and for being disinterested
in the "do-nothing" patient council. When a resident confronted him with his own behavior, the supervisor cau-
tioned the resident against "identifying with the patients," suggesting that this was part of the resident's own
"trouble with authority." And so it goes.

If therapists could only be more honest! But they/we
are not. Pretending to know more than we do, we dis-
simulate and fake things. When we forget the name of
someone's brother, we smile and nod, but don't ask.
When we forget someone's dream, we act as if we
remembered it. We act as if any fallibility on our parts is
fatal. Clients and patients, expecting the expertise the
profession itself insists on, defines, proclaims, and pretends to have—refuse to see therapists as human, even
when the therapists try to admit their own weaknesses.
The clients, then, collaborate in their own mystification,
not believing that a therapist could actually mean co is

simply human. The end result is that few people in therapy are honest about what they think and feel.

If therapists could be honest about being people with a skill trying to help other people, and if clients could say this is all they really want, then therapy as a *human* process could progress. The "profession" as such would crumble. We would all be "therapeutic" to one another. In this sense, therapy would be involved with social process and social change. It would deal with people's social and personal needs, with their feelings and interaction, and not with a jumble of diagnoses, techniques, and ambitions. But so long as therapy remains an establishment institution, mystified and sold on the open market, it will reinforce the status quo.

Therapy's model makes it invincible. Attempts to change training programs from within can be attacked as "acting out" or as "psychopathology," although the same programs put forward by administrators are lauded as innovative and far reaching. Unless they are backed by a client or other interest group, or are prepared to act together, young therapists can never get the necessary leverage to unseat those at the top. But the trainees, as well as the public, are mystified. They believe what they are told about how much learning, experience, special training, is needed to be a therapist. Trainees and lay people are viewed as fools. This is why we must shatter the myth of special skills, of professionalism, and open up this human activity to the people.

Therapy dehumanizes both trainees and patients/clients. The young therapist, like the young doctor, learns to accept it, to identify with it, to remold cos self-image in accordance with it. Thus, training institutions prepare therapists for the affluent classes, administrators for community (colonial) programs, researchers for drug teams, and teachers for more therapists. Therapists rehearse these skills on the poor clinic patients, often black or brown, and then go off to the suburbs to serve the affluent white. This is the racism and imperialism of therapy practice. This too is why non-middle-class people suspect and distrust therapists and don't accept their "neutrality" or "objectivity."

WE ARE ALL POTENTIAL PATIENTS, ALL POTENTIAL THERAPISTS

Once it is understood that we are all patients, all possible therapists, we are all people with problems in living who can help one another, then therapy can become a human activity, and cease to be a professional role or skill.

People meet problems in living from many sources—from other people, at work, at home, from their own feelings, from the oppression they experience. Some, with more privilege or strength or adaptability, can sail through. Others, barraged constantly, are worn down in ways which stretch the gamut of human experience. Some people, wholly against the wall, go mad, go "crazy."

Some people, of course, seem to have been born damaged. They suffer from some as yet unexplained metabolic or chemical or genetic/physical disorder that makes them "psychotic." A certain percentage of the population presumably is born with at least a genetic penchant for becoming crazy. Many other cultures deal with these people by providing a meaningful place for them. Our culture sends them to mental hospitals for their entire lives, electroshocks them into submissive numbness, or bludgeons their brains with chemicals. We don't know what to do with "organically" psychotic people. We suggest allowing the community to deal with them, without ostracizing them or handing them over to the pill pushers and shockers.

But it's the others we're most concerned with here—the people who span the entire range of human experience. Here we would introduce another concept: We all have a potential for many different human experiences. We can fall in love, go crazy, enjoy art and music, become outraged, turn sullen and despondent, cry, feel devastated or joyous, be totally "into our heads," and so on. In this omnipotentiality, madness and various kinds of emotional problems are all present.

Some people live under conditions that narrow down and channel their potential: being poor, being a victim of racism or sexism, having a tyrannical and sadistic parent. Very early in the game, then, some become "character types." They close off many of their potential options and experiences, and are reduced to a "type"—passive-aggressive, paranoid, and so on. This says something about our society's way of closing people off early on in their lives, of brutalizing them before they've had a chance to sprout beginnings, tentacles into the world.

For example, one patient had been brutalized both by an alcoholic, rejecting father, himself the victim of unemployment and low self-esteem, and by an overworked, angry, resentful mother whose life was a constant struggle to keep her head above water. Every time the patient asserted himself, he was shot down, punished, and told that it was ridiculous for him to expect to get anywhere in the world because no one could. Thus his parents passed their learning on to him. He too developed a sense of himself as nothing, as a failure. He too began expressing his anger at others, thus getting into trouble and confirming his picture of himself. By the time he was a teenager, he had already set a pattern of failure and frustration. He felt worthless but always angry and explosive; he had "paranoid" feelings of others' controlling his life, and fantasies of *really* being someone great and powerful, but in disguise. He was well on his way to being a chronic patient.

All of us have the potential for growth and creativity, for sharing our feelings with others. Even in those who have been brutalized, some part of this potential remains. It's this potential we need to develop. We need to build on people's strength and combat their weaknesses one by one. We need to analyze the conditions which create our weaknesses and to change those conditions. Understanding that people always have a potential for growth and change, if the conditions permit, we need to explore ways to elicit this potential.

Therapy is a human activity, relying on human skills. Therapists have preempted these skills, mystified and monopolized them, and forbidden others to develop them. This shouldn't blind us to the fact that the skills belonged to all of us to begin with, and are not the property of the therapy elite. The programs, as they currently exist, are oppressive institutions. They should, instead, be open institutes for the people, under community control and direction, available for training those with therapy potential, and for serving those in need.

The recent development of Insane Liberation of Mental Patients' Liberation Fronts is encouraging. It means that the "consumers" of therapy are getting together to share their experience, to develop "consumers' rights," and to make the therapy system more responsive to them, in fact, to bring it under their control. For centuries, mental patients' rights have been trampled and ignored; for years, the care of mental patients has been ludicrous and denigrating. The protest has come. Therapists, clients, and others should find out more about such ILF groups, and support them.[2]

That we are all potentially therapists does not mean that we should all be full-time therapists. Hopefully, in a new society, people will all be therapists with one another—i.e., be open, loving, and supportive—and so hav-

[2]Lists of these groups appeared in *Rough Times* (Box 89, Somerville, Mass. 02144) vol. 3, no. 2 (November 1972).

ing therapists as specialists in living problems will no longer be necessary. This, however, remains to be seen. For the present, people should be free to develop their own potential. Those who find that they have a natural skill for understanding people's feelings and situations and for helping them clarify and solve their interpersonal and emotional problems should have a chance to develop that skill. That's what demystification is all about: sharing what you know with people who want to know it, and who show that they can use the information. Information should serve the people.

We're saying some simple things: (1) therapy is a human activity; (2) therapy skills are human skills; (3) we are all patients; and (4) we are all potential therapists. Beneath this is a view of the world as changing, of life as constant flux with constant chance for growth. Oppression limits and kills us, alienates us from our bodies and minds and from our fellow people. Oppression puts us into diagnostic categories. Liberation would establish our potential again, in a social order that would respond to our human needs.

Why is it so hard to bring such simple truths into the open? Because therapists and the public alike are taught that there are special skills which therapists alone somehow possess. They are not taught that therapists have only *claimed* certain human skills for themselves and monopolized their use. Therapy itself has seemed an inappropriate subject for analysis. The fact is that what we have been taught is irrelevant and destructive. Our notions of therapy are obsolete. They are elitist, male-centered, obsessional, fear-ridden, and pessimistic. Our teachers have been opposed to substantial change. For they have been part of the ruling elite. They own property and securities and are heavily indentured for their work, prestige, and life style in the status quo. All change that liberated anyone would be at their expense. They would lose this status, the public's unchallenging deification of them, and blind acceptance of what they say. Our modes of practice—individual or community, group, family, and so forth—are racist and exploitative. The mystery which surrounds therapy makes it very hard to demand changes. Yet changes must be made.

THERAPY IS CHANGE

One of the worst features of psychological thought during these past decades has been its opposition to all notions of change. Much of this came from Freud's pessimism; much is simply built into the obsessional character of most therapists. A lot is dependent on therapists' class position and self-interest: Social and political changes threaten therapists more than patients.

And yet we all have the potential to change. We are not products of our past but only its prisoners. We have the potential to be different with different people, to change patterns we've lived by because other things become more important to us. When we are oppressed, though, we become pigeonholed, victimized, forced to live like nonpeople, alienated. We become the mental patients that the media tell us about. But this isn't necessarily the way it has to be. As Frantz Fanon has said:

I am not a prisoner of history. I should not seek there for the meaning of my destiny. . . . In the world through which I travel, I am endlessly creating myself.[3]

Fanon also suggests how therapy might be integrated into a revolutionary life. In *A Dying Colonialism*, he discusses the role of European doctors in Algeria. These landowners, consorts of the army, oppressors, were never

[3]Frantz Fanon, *Black Skin, White Masks* (New York: Grove Press, 1967), p. 229.

32

trusted by the Algerian people. Even their medical activity was suspect. They informed to the army; they were contemptuous and arrogant. They were, in fact, the enemy. In the struggle for independence, the Algerian people dealt with the matter of health-care specialization in a revolutionary way:

Orders were given to medical students, nurses, and doctors to join the combatants. Meetings were organized among political leaders and health technicians. After a short time, people's delegates assigned to handle public health problems came and joined each cell. All questions were dealt with in a remarkable spirit of revolutionary solidarity.

There was no paternalism; there was no timidity. On the contrary, a concerted effort was made to achieve the health plan that had been worked out. The health technician did not launch a "psychological approach program for the purpose of winning over the underdeveloped population." The problem was, under the direction of the national authority, to supervise the people's health, to protect the lives of our women, of our children, of our combatants.

The Algerian doctor . . . was reintegrated into the group. Sleeping on the ground with the men and women of the *mechtas,* living the drama of the people, the Algerian doctor became a part of the Algerian body. There was no longer that reticence, so constant during the period of unchallenged oppression. He was no longer "the" doctor, but "our" doctor, "our" technician.[4]

Knowledge about medical care was made available to the people, new health workers were created, and the mystery and aura of the "doctor" faded away. We're not implying that therapy skills are as important to revolu-

[4]Frantz Fanon, *A Dying Colonialism* (New York: Grove Press, 1967), p. 141–142.

tionary work as medical skills; there's certainly a difference. Yet, some kind of experience is needed in helping collectives and groups survive their inner conflicts and tensions, and in helping workers for change with the living problems they will have. Following Fanon's model, to share therapy skills and cut away the myths about their difficulty, to challenge the belief that they need to be in experts' hands, is relevant work. It's a matter of the professionals deprofessionalizing themselves, and of others simply developing the skills which are theirs to begin with. The doctor/patient roles, never really appropriate in therapy, are indefensible politically.

Thus the aim of radical therapists should be an end to therapy programs as they now exist. Everyone therapeutic, no one a therapist!

The old issue of "professionalism" cripples our efforts. Therapists today are socially stamped as "qualified," as "skilled," and as "professionals." They may or may not really possess therapy skills. Many who have never seen a therapy institute may also possess these skills. The whole issue of professionalism fades once we realize that what we're talking about is simply a human skill.

Professionalism is making a living out of your role as one-up while oppressed, suffering people are one-down. Professionalism is living a role, not a life; it's being resistant to change and not giving reasons, but rather using psychological innuendo to put others down and insulate yourself. It's falling back on mumbo jumbo people can't understand, on concepts that don't even make sense and have long since been proven wrong. It's being patronizing, charitable, condescending. Professionalism is what training schools teach us is the proper *attitude* toward our patients/clients.

We must expose professionalism, demystify it. In Claude Steiner's terms, we must help make people *aware* of this part of their *oppression.*[5]

[5]Claude Steiner, through personal communication.—MG

I[6] can best talk from my own experience. The program I was trained in was good, with a fine reputation, good teachers, and wise and profound thinkers. Yet the entire structure of the program conditioned my fellow trainees and me for the life of an oppressor.

We were without substantial power in affecting our own training. We ourselves were raggle-taggle and disunited; many trainees were afraid to challenge the hierarchy because we stood to gain a lot financially from going through the program quietly. We practiced what we learned on clinic patients and on various elements of the poor and minority groups who came into the hospital. We did "evaluations" time and again even though we knew we were unable to offer treatment for what we evaluated. Often we'd wind up referring people elsewhere for another evaluation period. We were told, though, that the evaluation was good for the patients and valuable for us as a prime learning activity. Our focus, in fact, was on learning psychopathology and psychodynamics, not on assisting our patients/clients.

Our orientation was predominantly individualistic. We were not taught much about families, groups, or communities, and nothing about the finances of therapy care and systems. We learned nothing about sociology, politics, anthropology, psychology (because we were in psychiatry), or the humanities.

We spent a lot of time reinforcing one another's stereotypes about men's and women's behavior and getting ready for Big Things—money, prestige, writing. We disliked being bullied by our supervisors, but we felt that all we had to do was hold on a bit longer.

We were politically naïve, unwilling to fight our own oppression. When Rick Kunnes was fired from the program, his colleagues were not willing to stand up with

[6]Throughout the book "I" refers to Michael Glenn.

him and demand an open hearing. Many of the residents, in fact, went along with their superiors' rumors about why Rick was being dismissed. We were unwilling to recognize that therapy was not a branch of medicine or social science, but a simply human activity in its own right.

New training programs must be developed. The old ones are working too well in subtly conditioning people to be oppressors. Features of a new program would have to include:

1. People will be considered without labels. The divisive distinctions between social worker, psychiatrist, and so on will be abolished; degrees will not matter. What will matter will be people's ability to relate to others and to their social and personal realities.

2. Programs will be open to everyone, hopefully funded by the communities they serve.

3. There will be no professional mystique; therapists will be workers like other workers. No one will get rich from other people's suffering, or command a ridiculous amount of prestige.

4. Hierarchies will give way to collective programs shaped by those who are trained and those who are served.

5. People will try different models of collective practice, new techniques, new living arrangements. Therapy care will be free and freely available. Therapists and clients will be from the same community.

Mystification   Therapists are in the dark about what they are supposed to do, about who they are. They hide behind intellectual stereotypes, armed with all sorts of theories—the more obscure the theory the better the dissimulation. The fact that they are experts at something they're not too clear about is the most important feature they have to disguise. They also have to conceal the fact that almost anyone can be therapeutic with others and that vital skills can be taught more quickly and more effectively, by far, than is currently being done.

Alienation All people in this society are alienated from their work, except of course the ruling class. Neither therapists nor their patients know where they fit into things. Not only are people alienated from their labor, they are alienated from one another, from the world around them, and from themselves. The various splits which develop in our Western capitalist countries are the objective basis for much of our cultural schizophrenia: divisions between aspects of our lives, between mind and body, ourselves and others, our inner and outer selves. By maintaining an "objective," detached role, therapists merely perpetuate this alienation, which drives people mad. Therapists who have been trained to be detached and clinical are even more alienated. They remain observers of, not participants in, the whole of life.

Oppression Therapists, not understanding the relation of their good-intentioned actions to the stability of this society, manage to take part in the oppression of those who are already most oppressed. Treatment techniques, the indignity of therapy, the loss of civil rights, the intimidation and psychological put down, the sexism and racism, are all a cherished part of conventional treatment. In the air force, I was stationed in a town with one psychiatrist. Treatment was a combination of electroshock, up drugs and down drugs, talking, and anything else available. None of this assault was questioned; it was something everyone was *grateful* for.

Oppression also derives from the fact that therapists had to go without things while they were being trained. They feel they have a right to them once they're finished. Thus the money gouging and rigid social attitudes. The primacy of *individual* concerns, *individual* solutions is everywhere.

Intimidation Therapists have been fired after

becoming involved in community politics. So long as therapists do what they're supposed to do, everything is OK. When they start understanding that *therapy is change, not adjustment,* and acting on this awareness, they get into trouble. No wonder many oppressed people mistrust therapists.

Status   The therapist has high status, exchangeable on the open marketplace for money, prizes, and a comfortable life. The pecking order of therapists is well established, and helps structure the guild. The status of therapists in the open society supports their prestige as long as they behave correctly. Even when one does not do the "right things," co is rarely arrested and smashed; rather co is left alone without the higher rewards of the profession.

Who Needs Medical Training?   Psychiatrists use their M.D. degrees to oppress other therapists and claim first place in the therapy sweepstakes. What exactly does medical school give? A lot of biochemistry, anatomy, physiology, urology, surgery, and so on, much of which is forgotten quickly. Much of it has to be consciously unlearned.

Repression   In most therapy training centers, the trainees are repressed, powerless. Their curriculum is not their own; their routine is set up by others. Theirs is not to question, but to follow and accept. It is amazing how readily most trainees tend to accept their superiors' view of them and abandon activism in favor of a search for the sickness within themselves. This is the result of mystification combined with the promise of grand rewards for accepting the status quo. In my experience, most therapist-trainees would not oppose a system that was treating them badly; rather, they would tend to endure it until they could reach the top themselves. That is, their salvation is linked to their future capacity to brainwash, co-opt, alienate, and mystify others. They rationalize in order to preserve their sense of integrity. But day after day, their original visions are eaten away. This repression of trainees maintains the system that serves therapists, not clients.

Politics Therapists are politically naïve, and their education does not equip them to understand the social and political implications of their work. By the time they do understand what's really happening, they'd rather not. The reasons for this are to be found in the class nature of American therapy and in the analysis of classes in our society.

3

Evolution of Therapy under United States Capitalism: Medical and Professional Models

Our major theme here is that therapy is part of and strongly supports the U.S. ruling class, its imperialist system, and the oppressive institutions which uphold it. When therapy isn't specifically supporting that system, it's supporting itself. The history of U.S. therapy mirrors the history of U.S. capitalism and imperialism, from the individual entrepreneur selling private practice to the large-scale social control of the masses.

HISTORY OF THERAPY IN THE UNITED STATES: MEDICAL HIERARCHY

Therapy as such in the United States began in the early nineteenth century with physicians as the first official therapists. Emotional problems were seen then as some kind of curse, the result of bad living, abnormalities in the brain and nervous system, or evil humors circulating in the body. In the early 1800s, the progressive elements in medicine began to "free" mental patients from their

40

chains. Pinel in France and Tuke in England regarded mental patients as human beings and tried to treat them rather than contain and imprison them. They released them from asylums and tried through various techniques to change their behavior. This was essentially an extension of the great bourgeois-democratic revolutions to the field of mental illness. From the start, medical personnel took charge of this movement. Physicians were the heads of asylums and ultimately became custodians of the interred masses, creators of the mammoth diagnostic systems, and the elite which was delegated supervisory power over the "insane" by the rest of society.[1] The organic approach to mental "illness" (i.e., something wrong with the body was causing problems in the head) became a new area of study in the field.

Other kinds of counseling had gone on before, of course, and continue to go on now. Clergy, quacks, faith healers, friends, and a whole variety of individuals promising aid for the distressed offered their services; and, by and large, they were accepted as legitimate by the less privileged segments of society.

The early U.S. asylum system consisted of places with a large staff and few patients—usually from well-to-do families. Therapy consisted of various treatments—hydrotherapy, simple talks, work, fear, whirlabouts in a chair, showers, and so on. The cure rate was actually fairly good.

In the decades after the Civil War, however, the population of the United States changed. Many more immigrants and poor people flocked to the cities, and gradually the lunatic asylums became storage bins for a variety of people. Many did not speak English, or respond to the "moral" (middle-class) treatment offered. Cure rates dropped, and the asylums became huge custodial centers,

[1]For a really fine presentation of this, see Michel Foucault, *Madness and Civilization* (New York: Pantheon, 1969).

still under strict medical control. This phenomenon was occurring also in Europe. It was during this time that psychiatry began to emerge as a medical specialty, akin to and an offshoot of neurology, and that the great textbooks of descriptive psychiatry were written.

A major change in this trend came at the turn of the twentieth century with the advent of psychoanalysis. The analysts pursued a theory of inner conflict: They felt that the madman's (and, more often, neurotic patient's) symptoms were traceable to the internal conflicts co faced, and that treatment could proceed by dealing with these conflicts. This was the beginning of the "psychodynamic" approach.

Freud and his colleagues treated people outside of hospitals. They did not treat the psychotic, interred people, but rather disturbed but somewhat functional, middle-class people. A whole sector of the intellectual and avant-garde as well as well-to-do clients now flocked to "therapy." The psychoanalyst became a major cultural figure. Freud's visit to the United States in the early part of the century, and the later immigration of many anti-Fascist psychoanalysts, strongly influenced American psychiatry. And because psychiatry was at the top of the therapy hierarchy, psychoanalysis became the major theoretical viewpoint which therapists learned to follow.

Still, physicians were in control. But now there was a split between the psychoanalytically oriented proponents of intrapsychic conflict and the more medically minded psychiatrists of the older physical/organic schools. The latter were usually employed in the asylum/state hospital system, and the former collected in large cities and universities where they taught and influenced the future course of their specialty. This split persists.

The analysts were progressive for their time. They challenged the assumption that mental patients' symptoms were somehow not understandable and continued the humanist-democratic attitude toward patients. Gradually, though, they became dogmatic and conservative, and their theory more and more detached from practice, more diffuse and abstract, and less relevant to anything. Because of this abstractness, errors in their theory could not be readily corrected; new analysts had to accept their false notions, which only a wave of ideological protest would later expose.

As the twentieth century progressed, people other than physicians got into the therapy scene. Soon after World War II, therapy suddenly came of age. Psychiatrists and psychologists were hired to sell bourgeois psychology to everyone, and the government suddenly discovered the value of the idea of "mental illness." Therapy was served up as a "comment on all," a cure-all. Social workers, clinical psychologists, hospital personnel, and others now claimed a special expertise all their own. Therapists became consultants to every sector of American life. Psychologists began to develop their own "clinical" talents, and social workers did the same. In fact, each group of ancillary personnel began to develop its own ideology, its own professional history, and its own "expertise."

Especially after 1963, when the mental health center program was proposed as a massive new attack on mental illness, jobs in the therapy field mushroomed. Although the medical model has been challenged from within the field, the professional aura of the therapist has, if anything, grown. Even the wild therapists, lay therapists, encounter therapists, and so on, see themselves as professional and benefit from the therapy mystique. There seems to be enough loot in America for all the therapists. Although there's a pecking order, the groups don't make war on one another; rather, they divide up the pie. Current trends include the pursuit of insurance monies paid for mental illness, "community" work, even packaged therapy franchises which sell therapy by the hour like boxes of fried chicken. Each new group of insurgent therapists has been bought off by the system's promise of prestige, money, jobs, and influence. This is the capitalist way: Those who sell a commodity in demand have their own way.

Any system of therapy has an impact on the distribution of power within society. All behavior, therapeutic or otherwise, has both political implications and consequences. In the politics of therapy—the power relationships of therapy—the therapists in general and the psychiatrists (M.D.s) in particular are in charge. The medical model predominates. That is, there is a *patient* with a *disease* manifested by various *symptoms* which are to be treated by a *physician* (or at least supervised by a physician) in a *clinic* or *hospital*, often with *medicine.* As long as this medical model prevails, physicians will be at the top of the heap in terms of power, prestige, and profits. Virtually all government funds for therapy go to physician-dominated mental health programs. It was only because physicians feared the competition of too many psychiatrists that until the late 1960s, they opposed any move to increase the number of medical schools, physicians, and ultimately psychiatrists. It is only because "mental health" needs are too pervasive to be dealt with by physicians alone that nonphysicians have become part of mental health service centers at all. Even so, such centers still do not significantly improve any community's mental health.

The therapist always has some preconceived notion as to what is good for people. Thus co can't avoid imposing cos values upon cos clients. The issue then is what those values are, in what political context they fit, and whether they are politically (or morally) correct.

Today therapy is big business, a growth industry. Psychiatrists who want to serve as administrators in the new mental health centers can command a large salary. There is room for a whole assortment of therapists—psychologists, art therapists, occupational therapists, social workers, family specialists, and so on—all making a handsome living off the people. The mental health boom has created vast numbers of jobs—for professionals and even a few privileged nonprofessionals.

The values and aims of the therapy business are those of our society. Just as the hospital physicians are seen as elite professional custodians of the sick—in truly liberal, humanitarian fashion—so the private practitioners are seen as quasi-gurus, magical healers possessed of strange aura and medicine: the answers to everyone's woes.

Therapy services now span a wide gamut from private practitioner to the business-military consultant, to the shrink in the community mental health center, to the head of the traditional wards in state mental hospitals. They embrace the old entrepreneurial (early capitalist) model as well as the new corporate liberalism of the mental health center movement, and thus are closely allied to mental health imperialism—i.e., pillaging and control of masses of poor and third world peoples, the use of therapy as a means of social conditioning and manipulation, or as a means of intimidation and punishment (as in commitment, electroshock, forced tranquilization).

It is this growing tendency of therapy to serve the ruling class that concerns us here. For it increasingly eradicates therapy's all too tiny progressive aspect, and makes it a willing ally in the oppression of masses of people. Thus, the new therapy leads to a "team" of corporately functioning elites—urbanologists, economists, architects, penologists—not only to the entrepreneurial therapist. The agents of change are the corporate team, not an individual shrink.

Long and expensive training, of course, insures that therapists will be available only in limited numbers; thus competition is limited, and the few therapists available are white and from upper- and middle-class backgrounds.

Like other medical specialties, psychiatry (and the various kinds of therapy which model themselves after psychiatry) trains therapists to treat the upper and middle classes (in private practice) by practicing and experimenting on poor and working people. This is health imperialism. Its widespread appearance in the United States is directly linked to imperialism, and to therapy's part in that system.

None of this is meant to suggest that therapists are more power hungry or profit mad than other groups of professionals and privileged elites. Services controlled by them, though, ultimately serve ruling-class interests, not those of the masses in need of relevant treatment. The medical/professional model makes it certain that genuine therapy is withheld from the masses, and that a phony therapy (social control with a sweet veneer) is liberally bestowed upon them to keep them in their places.

THERAPY AS POLITICALLY REPRESSIVE

Because patients are encouraged to be introspective and to spend time examining their own consciences, they are steered away from confronting political issues. In fact, if they even examine the political context, patients are accused of "avoidance," and thus one more symptom is added to the constellation of "presenting problems." Implicit in therapy is the assumption that the sociopolitical system is adequate or perhaps needs only a few small reforms, and that it is the patients who are inadequate and must more than reform their ways.

If politics deals with power, then the therapist must always deal with politics. Therapists encourage patients either to accept the existing distributions of power in their environment or to change them, whether that power distribution be between individuals, families, communities, or countries. In practice, professional activities

46

designed to change the status quo are political and therefore "unprofessional"; activities designed to strengthen the status quo are, of course, "medical" or "neutral" or "therapeutic."

Right-wing civil libertarians like Thomas Szasz are libertarians and not revolutionaries because their notion of freedom includes free enterprise system, or marketplace. This stance is no less repressive than that expressed by conventional therapists. In effect, both groups deny that all forms of therapy are institutionalized and must ultimately serve America and hence be repressive.

It is questionable whether we will need or want therapists in postrevolutionary society. Not that there won't be people suffering from anxieties and depression, but it will be recognized that the best way to deal with these symptoms is through the political group or collective of which the individual is a member: People will engage in criticism/self-criticism on a unity/struggle/unity model. The ultimate result of a therapy based on a mythical political neutrality is to conceal the existence of political conflicts and struggle and to strengthen the status quo.

Another result of the medical model is the patient who is labeled "sick" loses any legitimacy, political or social, in talking about or dealing with political issues. Co is defective, a nonperson, not to be believed or trusted. Indeed, many therapists attempt to avoid political issues altogether by saying that the purpose of their therapy is simply to "strengthen" the client. But of course what the therapist winds up strengthening are those characteristics which most support the status quo.

By undergoing "successful" therapy, a person who might have been angry and have confronted the status quo is made to feel comfortable within it. Defusing even one person's political militancy may have profound political consequences.

Many therapists believe that the therapeutic encounter is still the best means by which people can be helped to feel better and to learn to deal with their environment. In effect, such notions mystify patients' lives by encouraging them to believe that therapy can explain away and deal with what are ultimately complex political issues. Thus therapy hinders political growth.

In some cases, symptomatic therapies such as drug or behavior therapy may be more repressive or may follow more closely the medical model than traditional "insight" psychotherapy. Drug or behavior therapy focuses on specific symptoms and is analogous to symptomatic treatment of a medical disease. At least occasionally "insight" therapy may deal with the broader aspects of a person's life, rather than with an isolated "sickness." In the medical model, symptomatic treatment involves the psychotherapist's becoming a surgeon and removing the diseased piece of behavior, the symptom. Broader-based conventional therapies might at least emphasize that symptoms arise from a complex interaction of personal, social, and environmental factors, and are not isolated phenomena that must be excised before anyone asks—or might learn—why they occurred.

Any drug or therapy that makes a person feel better and does not change the objective conditions which created the "bad feelings" can easily lessen the person's motivation to confront and challenge an oppressive situation. By prescribing a drug or a certain symptom-relieving therapy for a client, the therapist is usually implying that the patient's "diseases" are internal and not sociopolitically based. In effect, following the medical model, a person who needs pills is judged to be sick and a sick person is judged to need pills—either way it's almost a self-fulfilling prophecy. The radical therapist might use tranquilizers to take the edge off some anxiety, but then the ultimate political causes of the anxiety—and the fact that the pill is not meant to deal with those issues—must be clearly explained to the client.

Any therapist who wishes to be more than an agent for

social control must have some sense of the political outcomes of therapy—i.e., is the patient made more or less militant, more or less politically conscious? To evaluate such an outcome and to guide the patient in the most politically left direction, the therapist, of course, must have cos politics together. (Obviously, not *all* patients *want* to be left or "radical" or revolutionary, and the therapist, radical or otherwise, should not attempt to *force* the patient to become politically active.)

Drug companies encourage psychiatrists and patients to deal with problems according to the medical model—i.e., "a pill for every ill." In fact, greedy drug companies are pushing pills or at least want pills (tranquilizers, in this case) pushed not only by nonpsychiatric physicians, but also by nurses and various other aides. Certainly, nonpsychiatric physicians and mental health aides *can* be taught to prescribe safely and effectively. Nevertheless, under current circumstances, not only are psychiatrists often poorly informed about drugs, but worse, they receive no training or an antitraining about the political implications of drug therapy. The same is true with nonpsychiatric physicians and mental health aides—which is precisely the way the drug companies want it. They want the pills pushed in political ignorance. To lose that ignorance would raise questions about motives and profits of the drug company.

PSYCHIATRY AND THE U.S. POLITICAL-ECONOMIC SYSTEM

The United States is the bastion of world capitalism/imperialism. Just as our economy has historically evolved along capitalistic lines, so has psychiatry evolved from the entrepreneurial, laissez-faire model of the private practitioner to the corporate liberalism of the community mental health center. In the old psychiatry, the "adjuster" was the psychiatrist alone in cos private office. In the new community psychiatry, however, the "adjuster" is a team of corporately functioning elites. The prominent theories of psychiatry and mental health have evolved from psychoanalysis to modern systems analysis.

Just as our economy and politics have become dominated by the mechanisms of the military-industrial complex, so the mental health market is dominated by similar mechanisms. First is their common emphasis on pacification and counterinsurgency. Second, just as the defense industry is really a war industry, so the mental health market is really a mental illness market. Third, defense depends on war, or the threat of war; mental health depends on mental illness. Both need an influx of federal money to stabilize their financial bases.

Much of the current intraprofessional feuding is between the old line, laissez-faire, isolationist, financially independent solo-practitioner and the modern, corporate liberal, community mental health specialists who are dependent on the U.S. Treasury. Although the debate focuses on professional technology and skills—i.e., couches versus community centers, psychoanalysts versus systems analysts, and so on—the real issue, namely that mental health programs and priorities are defined according to economic factors, not therapeutic efficacy, remains undiscussed.

No matter what stage of psychoeconomic evolution we're in, psychiatry serves the system and its norms. Community mental health aims at the systematic subordination of individual behavior to false social norms. For example, look at some of the roles psychiatry plays in the following settings.

Schools   Psychiatrists or community health specialists serve the school not the students. They label as "sick" or "problems" certain students or groups of students, never the school administration or the politicoeconomic system in which it functions. That the school is a mindless and alienating, racist and sexist tracking system for the military-industrial complex is never seriously examined. Such an examination calls for a political response, not a psychiatric one. Not to examine these issues is to "rationalize," in the Rand Corporation sense of the word, the school system.

Police Police departments increasingly are allying themselves with academic departments of psychiatry for assistance in dealing with individual offenders, crowd control, and "conflict resolution." In effect, staff members of community mental health programs, and psychiatrists, under the guise of "medical methods," serve as public relations experts for one of our most repressive institutions. If not directly working for city police, psychiatrists and other community mental health specialists will be using their skills for purposes of social control. Thus, a past president of the American Medical Association, in addition to the chairman of a psychiatry department, jointly called for psychiatrists systematically to collect basic behavioral data on all U.S. citizens so that the community psychiatrist could forecast and control "behaviors of populations under a variety of circumstances."[2]

Corporations Corporations and the military use therapy in much the same way. It's no coincidence that the most liberal of corporations, IBM, is also one of the first to provide on-the-job psychiatric services. The goal, of course, is to maximize worker productivity (if people's needs are met, it's accidental). Dr. E. Ginzburg, a medical economist at Columbia University School of Business, advises that a corporation's psychiatric service should not attempt to deal with psychosis because it doesn't respond quickly and "economically" to treatment; the employer, he believes, should be "circumspect" and not throw good money after bad.[3] The Soviet Union, using systems analysis and cost-accounting procedures very similar to our

[2]Morris Fishbein, *Medical World News*, June 15, 1969, p. 85.
[3]E. Ginzburg, *Men, Money, and Medicine* (New York: Columbia University Press, 1969), pp. 244–246.

Defense Department's, has shown that their on-the-job psychiatric programs save millions of dollars a year. Industrial corporations are loath to provide services that might not improve productivity. Even for executives, encounter-type therapies were abandoned in many corporations when successful authoritarian types came back less authoritarian and less dogmatic and also less productive—even though they were more comfortable with themselves and others. Psychology and psychiatry are increasingly used for purposes ranging from selling deodorants to isolating and repressing those who step to a different drummer (or worse yet, who have dreams of a better society).

Elsewhere, psychiatrists are helping corporations diversify. For example, Lockheed and Raytheon, two of the major defense contractors, unhappy with their images as war makers, have moved into a popular and profitable new business. Guided by community psychiatrists, these corporations are developing special teaching films and programmed learning devices aimed at dissuading high school students from taking drugs. The films emphasize the establishment's ideology that drugs lead to the ruin of reputation, career, and property. Community psychiatrists are thus providing the linkages between the military-industrial complex and the medical-industrial complex.

Prisons and the Military In these institutions, total, unquestioning obedience is demanded, and many methods, from persuasion to isolation to physical punishment, may be used on recalcitrant prisoners (or soldiers). The therapist is just a more refined instrument for obtaining absolute submission. Cos therapy serves one end alone— to break the resistance of those on whom other, more direct, methods have failed, and to ease the way to "adjustment" (i.e., submission) for all. The therapist can see cos patients only as criminals and never as political prisoners.

Psychiatry and psychology are thus used as direct instruments of coercion against individuals; under the guise of "medical treatment," people are pacified, punished, or incarcerated. But psychiatry and psychology are also used more generally as instruments of pacification and control of our entire society. They have become a central ideological instrument for obscuring people's understanding of their experience and for preventing their recognizing the social bases and collective nature of their oppression.

The central mechanism by which psychiatry and psychology achieve this end is to reduce all collective experience to a sum of individual experiences, to reduce all social grievances to individual pathology. Psychiatrists are trained to try to impose the responsibility for a patient's problem on the patient coself, rather than on cos environment. The March 1970 issue of *TransAction* published an article by Thomas J. Scheff on this process: "Most psychotherapists have been trained to view patients as favorable candidates for psychotherapy if they have insight into their illness—which is to say that they accept, or can be led to accept, their problems as internal."[4]

Morals   Therapists have been defining and defending the morals of the system. For example, they have encouraged monogamy, male supremacy, and heterosexuality, at the same time labeling everything else "deviant." Whether the therapist admits it or not, at every point in the therapeutic program, whether in his office or the community, co prescribes a set of values that in turn describes and supports the establishment's moral-political stance.

Women's Oppression   One of the most pervasive uses of therapy for oppression is to subjugate women. A woman is told that her failure to accept her prescribed

[4]Thomas J. Scheff, "Being Mentally Ill," *TransAction* 7, no. 5 (June 1970): 244–246.

roles of housekeeper, nursemaid, and husband pamperer results from her own psychological inadequacies as mother and wife, not from flaws in the institutions of marriage and the family and in the roles defined within them. If she fails to wipe Con Ed's soot off the window sills every day, she is a "bad" housekeeper; if her child uses dope to escape the emptiness and despair of the streets, she is a "bad" mother. Whether delivered in person by her psychiatrist, or through the mass psychotherapy of Abby, Ann Landers, Rose Franzblau, and the *Reader's Digest*, the message is clear: Your oppression as a woman is your fault, not a social problem. It's an issue of mental illness, not a derivative of economic exploitation; hence it must be met individually (by changes in yourself), not collectively.

Attacking the New Left Therapists have sought to explain the rise of the New Left in terms of the psychology of the dissenters, not their politics. Vietnam, racism, poverty, imperialism disappear save as triggers of latent psychopathology. The *New York Times*, for example, called in psychiatrist David Abrahamsen, a specialist in the study of violence, to explain the politics which led up to a rash of bombings. The bombers need not be psychotic, he said; they may be dissatisfied persons with a grudge.[5] Such psychiatric descriptions have found expression in the plans of the Nixon administration for increased surveillance and repression of the left. One "highly placed Nixon assistant" described extreme radicals thus: "It wouldn't make a bit of difference if the war or racism ended overnight. We're dealing with the criminal mind, with people who have snapped for some reason."[6]

The New York *Daily News* cast the idea into lay peo-

[5]Editorial, *Bulletin of the Health Policy Advisory Center,* May 1969, p. 3.
[6]Ibid.

54

ple's language—"spoiled, self-centered brats" who "hate everything decent and good."[7] The therapists give the same theme the respectability of science. Widely publicized in the mass media, their views help shape the public's consciousness of the movement. They help insulate the good TV-watching, *Readers' Digest*-reading citizens from understanding what the movement is all about, how it relates to the forms of oppression they feel in their own lives, and why they should take it seriously on its own terms.

For example, a few radical students will "trash" a building. The radicals' politics will be transformed into psychopathology and their oedipal complexes will be carefully examined in scores of scholarly papers. But President Nixon can inflict unimaginable horror throughout Southeast Asia, and no community therapist is consulted on his oedipal complex or psychopathology.

Oppression of Black and Third World People For every challenge from a black or Puerto Rican or Chicano or American Indian or Asian-American, there's a repressive answer from psychology and psychiatry. According to presidential advisor Daniel Moynihan, black riots are attributable to the "instability of the Negro family," not poverty and racism, hopelessness and anger.[8] Absenteeism among the blacks and Puerto Ricans in low-paying, dead-end jobs is due to inadequate socialization of the virtues of promptness and perseverance, not to the inhumanity and pointlessness of the jobs themselves. Acceptance of the status quo is normal and healthy; deviance in thought or behavior, whether individual or collective, is pathological. People are taught to think of themselves and the deviations and dissents of others in

[7]Ibid.
[8]Lee Rainwater and William Yancey, *Moynihan Report and the Politics of Controversy* (Cambridge, Mass.: MIT Press, 1967), pp. 292–295.

these terms. A sick society is transformed into nothing more than a collection of sick individuals.

Whether it be the "neurotic" housewife, "acting out" pupil, or the "paranoid student radical," therapy has become a central ideological instrument for obscuring people's understanding of their experience and for preventing their recognition of the social bases and collective nature of their oppression. It does this by reducing collective experience to a sum of individual experiences and by reducing all social grievances to individual pathology. Racism, sexism, exploitation, and imperialism disappear, save as triggers of latent psychopathology. Conceived of in scholarly journals, boiled down by pop psychiatrists, advice columnists, and consultants, therapy has become the pseudoscientific underpinning for a repressive ideology that promotes alienation from oneself, from others, and from reality.

Therapy is thus deeply involved in the oppression carried out every day by the few rich who run society on the minds and bodies of the working and poor people who create the country's wealth.

4

Community Therapy Exposed

We don't accept the genetic-factor view of emotional problems, nor do we see emotional problems as caused by people's own "fault," by their drifting downward due to inherent weaknesses. We see emotional problems as caused by a combination of extrinsic and intrinsic factors: Certain illnesses such as varieties of schizophrenia do indeed seem more linked to intrinsic factors; others such as reactive depression are certainly more linked to extrinsic events. Freudian psychology emphasized intrapsychic, intrinsic factors almost exclusively. We do not go along with this view or with its opposite, that of seeing all emotional suffering as extrinsically caused and mediated. To do either would be to indulge in gross one-sidedness. But we do feel that the extrinsic factors of life in a maddening society, of a cruel and genocidal system, strongly shape and injure each person living in this country.

The sex-role stereotypes, the pressure to conform, the pressure to excel, the packaging and dehumanization of intimacy, the acceptance of everyday violence, the incarceration of rebels: All these are facts of everyday life under U.S. capitalism. This is why the studies of Midtown USA show such a high percentage of "mental illness" among the population. People's lives are beyond their control; they are battered every day; they are denied their perceptions; they are humiliated and inundated by propaganda. All this is common knowledge.

If psychiatry serves the system and the system in turn causes mental disability, what is the community therapist to do? And more important, what is the community to do? Practicing community therapy in a conventional way in contemporary American society, especially in ghetto areas, is like practicing it in a concentration camp, even if co really meets some people's needs there and is supportive of them, co can function only as a part of the pacification program within the camp and thus can only support it. In such a political environment, the therapist's work is counter to the prisoners' most crucial and urgent needs, i.e., getting out of and causing the destruction of the camp. The concentration camp therapist, if co chooses to function in the camp in cos customary way, will have as cos first priority the meeting of personal and professional needs, i.e., to function as a traditional therapist, regardless of the political and social setting. This is to function in a totally corrupt fashion. The only responsible, socially utilitarian way co can function is to be a politicomilitary organizer or technician—all in the service of the destruction of the camp.

Yet this is not how community therapy works. Massive sums of money are being poured into community mental health centers in order to reach every person in this society. "Catchment areas" catch everyone. Police, schools, courts, parents, can send people in for checkups. The reactionary elements in the community wind up as trustees of the centers, and determine policy—to make war on pot, to get kids to conform, to control dissent, to tranquilize the agitated. And at the top of the structure, dispensing concern and conventional wisdom, stand the community therapists. Though they talk a liberal rap, community therapists are powerless to effect far-reaching social changes (they'd be fired); instead they help control and contain people.

As for community mental health services and programs, it must be noted that pragmatic decisions are made on virtually a totally materialistic basis. The "success," "failure," or survival of a particular mental health service has little or nothing to do with its health-enhancing qualities or therapeutic efficacy. Survival of a program is primarily determined by whether it enhances or protects its parent system's institutional and professional practices, its profits, prerogatives, and prestige. All too often the definition of community therapy as "those programs which keep the community safe for therapists," has become the reality of community mental health programs. Too many therapists and community mental health specialists seem to believe that the primary purpose of mental health programs is to prevent, rather than to foment, social action. As one past president of the American Psychiatric Association said: "Administrators and deliverers of mental health services will have to sharpen their perception and recognition of their responsibilities in *maintaining social homeostasis.* They bear a social responsibility much in the *same way as the courts and other law enforcement agencies do*" (emphasis added).[1]

The political value (i.e., value to the system) of a mental health program helps determine and define its success or failure. One example is the role of the community mental health center as a pacification program, particularly as "law and order" issues become more visible and viable, and it becomes politically more profitable to keep down the "natives." As J. M. Statman, a Washington D. C. psychologist, points out, pacification produced by the use of massive armed force "represents only one and not necessarily the most effective means of inducing obedience." It is often the employment of only minimal force "which

[1]Dr. Lawrence Kolb, *International Journal of Psychiatry* 9 (1969): 286.

proves to be the most effective. This may be especially true if such force is presented in a form that is not readily perceived as coercive or which, in fact, is seen as helpful in intent by both the agents of oppression and the oppressed. The mystification of experience which accompanies the acceptance of such 'kindness' creates a form of oppression far more destructive than that of the armed occupier." Thus, in the urban ghetto and elsewhere, it is the social worker, the psychologist, the educator, and the community therapist who play the key oppressive roles, who have become the "soft police."

Community mental health programs, in general, do serve to pacify a neighborhood—particularly a ghetto— and are thus functionally racist. The community mental health programs "mystify and mollify justifiable outrage and thereby prevent action for meaningful change." By directing community concern toward problems of "mental health" and away from "efforts to confront the basic oppressive institutions in our society, such programs function to maintain the establishment's status quo, rather than to advance the interests of the oppressed community."[2]

It thus appears that community mental health programs divert community energies from more meaningful efforts, that they depoliticize issues and instead "psychiatricize" them, that the employment of community leaders co-opts them and alienates them from their community and thereby weakens the community power base, and that such programs, no matter how good their intentions, cannot turn against their funding source and one of the major agents of community oppression: the government.

In the face of all the ballyhoo about community mental health, it is encouraging that many community programs

[2]J. M. Statman, "Community Mental Health as Pacification," *American Journal of Orthopsychiatry* 40, no. 4:393–95.

are now starting to experience a lack of patients! The communities served by these monsters are beginning to understand what they are all about. People come to the mental health center with one problem. This is ignored, and they are diagnosed as having another problem, and offered treatment for it—and usually humiliated. National minority groups are mistrustful of "therapy," as are the young, many women, gays. The commodity isn't selling so well. The therapists are sitting in their store, talking to one another. This trend has not yet been fully realized. In some parts of the country, for instance, working people's aversion to more traditional forms of therapy has been offset somewhat by increasing use of intimacy mills (encounter, family, and group therapy) by the alienated middle class. There is still money in the old well, you just have to dip in with the right bucket.

Community control must be seen in its broadest sense, namely where a community itself controls and determines its own political, social, and economic realities. We can't talk about community mental health without a community, and we can't talk about a community until it has a political consciousness of itself and controls itself. The fight for and the achievement of real control of the community, by and for the community, will ultimately determine just how therapeutic our communities can be. Let us clarify here that we are talking about control by poor and working people, by the working class and its allies, not by the middle class.

Therapists in community-controlled mental health services will not be allowed to practice in their customary fashion. Such a community will attempt to integrate all services into a human services network, including schools, fire departments, and police in order to eliminate professional and institutional priorities and biases.

One example of professional, establishment, and institutional imperatives holding sway over community need is the addiction crisis. Community therapists and other community mental health specialists view addiction as a personality problem and talk of the so-called addictive personality. However, there is a far greater correlation between addiction and economics and geographic distribution than with personality types. Yet, treatment programs are geared for changing individual personalities and not the political realities which are responsible for the addiction problems. The immediate political realities are the Mafia, police complicity, and political payoffs throughout the city. Professor R. Cloward of Columbia University notes that governmental inactivity and narcotics traffic are tolerated as long as they aid the establishment's status quo: "As long as slum dwellers remain on drugs they cannot mobilize politically."[3] The Black Panthers prohibit the use of narcotics for just that reason. Only the People's Defense Leagues' drug treatment programs are serious and efficacious; they alone relate to political realities. The people of these organizations know that the political system kills one hundred addicts per month in New York City alone. Thus, the violence is already there and the question of whether the Leagues' response should be violent, is academic. The People's Defense Leagues function as vigilante groups, shooting and killing major drug pushers on sight. The Leagues are having more therapeutic effects on the community in general and addicts in particular than any other extant treatment program. And to be sure, no community therapist ever thought of such a program or researched its possibilities, but people from the community did.

How can community control of mental health services be seriously effective if the community has no understanding of the theory of community therapy? Community control refers to the community's controlling the overall policies and priorities of the services. The commu-

[3] *New York Times,* May 13, 1969, p. 62.

nity through its elected board would make decisions about, for example, whether the treatment program should have a long-term, individual, psychoanalytic orientation; whether addiction services should be emphasized; or whether research and training programs should be emphasized over direct services. The community has not only a right to control its services (after all, as a minimum rationalization for community control, services for mental health are well over 50 percent publicly funded and thus should be publicly controlled), but also has a need and an ability to make decisions relevant to itself. It might require an "expert" to determine the relative harm of the side effects of Mellaril versus Thorazine, but a community can evaluate the overall relevance of various services offered.

Is there a danger in giving the "lay person" too much say? The danger is in not giving co, i.e., the community, enough. Without community control, services and professionals are accountable to no one; priorities are determined privately and secretly, and artificial hierarchies are maintained. More dangerous than not giving the community what it deserves, is the community's failure to demand and take what is its own. The professionals' attempts to deny the community its right of self-determination with the rationalization that the community may not be familiar with certain techniques and technology is akin to former President Johnson's ignoring the public's criticism of the Vietnam War because "the public doesn't have all the facts." It is not necessary to be a general in My Lai to know that the United States has no legitimate business in Vietnam. By the same token, one does not have to be a trained therapist to understand that long-term, individual, psychoanalytic therapy has little relevance to the community at large.

What will community control do about professionalism? Professionalism encourages artificial hierarchies, as well as personnel shortages. The professional earns more than the worker. The fight for deprofessionalization doesn't mean that everyone winds up with the same amount of knowledge and skills. We will always need a division of labor, where some technicians have some degree of expertise. but possession of expertise, according to the community, should in no way legitimize power to set policy and maintain privileges such as higher salaries.

Nobody is suggesting that there be no standards, say, for surgeons. What the community is saying and demanding is that these standards not be arbitrary and exclusionary, that they be based on fact and function, not on privilege, that they be open to public scrutiny and review, that there be different routes by which one achieves those standards—e.g., academic training versus on-the-job training with open-ended career ladders.

The ideal professional works to put cos professions out of business. For example, a doctor's ultimate goal should be to end all sickness and disability, so that the medical profession is no longer needed.

Individual "patients" acting alone, even with the financial resources of a national health insurance, cannot organize or demand services that are politically relevant and personally responsive. Only groups of working people and their allies can do that.

Community mental health training programs must be drastically altered and control of these programs removed from therapists. That is, those trained at our best university institutions have a limited understanding of how the human personality functions because their knowledge is based almost exclusively on a Freudian understanding of personality development—to the neglect of entire areas of knowledge in psychology, sociology, anthropology, economics, and political science.

The only answer to community mental health needs is for communities to control their own centers. This means that mental health should be the concern of patients' groups, local residents, and so forth. Halfway houses, day hospitals, therapy centers, and addiction services should all be run as community-based programs. As the community becomes more concerned with social change, its mental health programs will become more innovative and satisfying. In this sense, development of the revolutionary consciousness will lead to a more effective mental health program, better by far than the reformist offerings of the "progressive" mental health buffs. If the priority is change of mental health services, the services will be reformist. If the priority is a changed society, the services will participate in that movement.

5

Therapy and Sexism

Sexism is the oppression of one sex by the other: in our society, men oppressing women. The term also refers to the oppression of homosexuals by the heterosexual world. Sexism comes out of an unequal power relationship. The inequality is used to dominate further, to control or denigrate people already in a weaker position, to deepen the inequality.

In an oppressive society, all people bear marks of oppression. But certain groups, because of their nationality or sex or color, become more oppressed than others. For this reason—and because women make up more than 50 percent of our population—it is important to discuss sexism and its psychology. A similar discussion would hold for racism and the oppression of third world peoples in this country—and for imperialism and our country's exploitation of the rest of the world.

Much has been written recently about women's position in Western society, analyzing the economic/social/-political causes of their oppression, its psychological/sexual/interpersonal effects, and the alternatives open to women for changing the situation.[1] No woman growing

[1]Cf. Shulamith Firestone, *The Dialectic of Sex* (New York: Morrow, 1970); Robin Morgan, ed., *Sisterhood Is Powerful* (New

up in this society can escape sexism, even though some women have more privilege than others by virtue of their class position (or that of the men they become involved with).

Sexism revolves around the economic exploitation of women, leading to advantages for the bosses in our capitalist system, and around psychological/sexual exploitation, leading to advantages for all men over "their" women. Even in socialist countries, women can be exploited and oppressed unless efforts are made to change that situation directly. That is, sexism is linked to capitalism, but it will not be abolished by abolishing capitalism alone. The particular effects of sexism or racism need specific, conscious programs to overcome them.

Margaret Benston has pointed out how the economic exploitation of women is a fundamental feature of our society.[2] Unpaid household work creates a dichotomy between "real work," which men do for money, and "housework," which women do because they have to, for free (or for their own room, board, and allowance). Housework places the majority of women outside the money economy and deprives them of the status which comes to people earning money. It removes them from the organizable labor market and deprives them of political power such as that which working men have through their unions. Money is value, and being stuck with housework and child care gives women less value as people.

Years ago Friedrich Engels stated:

York: Random House, 1970); the packet of women's liberation articles available from the New England Free Press (791 Tremont Street, Boston, Mass.); and the periodicals *Everywoman, Off Our Backs, The Women's Page, Women: A Journal of Liberation.*

[2]Margaret Benston, "The Political Economy of Women's Liberation," *Monthly Review* (September 1969), available as a pamphlet for 10 cents from New England Free Press.

The first premise for the emancipation of women is the reintroduction of the entire female sex into public industry . . . the emancipation of women and their equality with men are impossible and must remain so as long as women are excluded from socially productive work and restricted to housework which is private.[3]

Part of this statement can be challenged. Women's work —housework and child rearing—is socially productive, but it is not remunerable and gives women no economic/political power. Even when women do enter the job market, they receive inferior jobs and inferior pay for equivalent work and have less opportunity for advancement than men. Their work is appropriated at as little cost as possible.

When women remain in nuclear families, they are defined by their relationship to their husbands (or fathers) —that is, most women are defined in terms of the men in their lives. This alienates women from themselves and from other women and makes them reflections of someone else. It also makes women tremendously vulnerable, for their survival depends on their continually pleasing the men from whom their social identity comes. If they do not cook well, satisfy them sexually, keep the house clean as demanded, they are in danger of being "replaced" by more efficient and more pleasing women. Thus, they must work hard at their unpaid tasks; isolated from one another, they are at men's mercy. In this society men, oppressed by their jobs and bosses and institutions, transfer their anger and frustration to their wives and children; they expect to be supported at home, not challenged. That too is women's role—emotional support of the men who dominate yet depend on them.

Women learn "survival techniques" to get along.

[3]Friedrich Engels, "Origin of the Family, Private Property, and the State," available from New England Free Press.

Knowing they must appeal to men, they learn to look sexy, flirt when it is appropriate, behave subserviently, cook and fuck well, care for children without complaining, clean their homes, shop thriftily, carry on pleasant conversation, listen to their men's complaints and support their sagging self-esteem even if it has to be at the expense of their own. That's "women's work." The mass media give her a hundred different hints regarding cooking, homemaking, sexual techniques, psychological understanding. Her early training, the images she grows up seeing on TV and in the newspapers and magazines, the high school courses she is expected to take, the popular songs she hears on the radio, all prepares her for a role as wife and mother, coating it in romantic expectation to insure a "proper" mental attitude toward the future. She has been raised to be retiring, shy, and feminine; a boy's aggressiveness has been encouraged, but a girl's has been cut down as unladylike. Tomboyish behavior is tolerated, but not past puberty. Girls have been brought up to be polite dolls, fashion models, sexual objects, and future baby factories. They learn by copying their unhappy mothers and elder sisters—often swearing to themselves that they will take a different path in their lives. But when few options arrive which can pull them from an oppressive home or from a boring, unrewarding life, they leap at the chance to get married. If she has learned well, a woman will be able to attract men, and probably even "catch" one and be taken care of for the rest of her life. Though she can never be free of the fear of being abandoned, she can at least build up some elements of security —clothes and furniture, a car perhaps, a wedding ring, the legal and psychological commitment of the marriage contract, a sense of her capacity to be attractive. If she has "professional" ambitions, she may be able to make it into a man's world and gain even more privilege—with the proper effort and luck. The basic fact, though, is that she continues to be defined on men's terms—whether it's in relation to the man she is living with, her job in a man's company, or the ability she has to fulfill her female stereotype in a man's world.

Men too worry about being abandoned in relationships; other men may "take" *their* women away. But a man's situation differs from a woman's in several ways. A man whose woman leaves him usually retains job security, a higher earning potential than the woman, social mobility, and a sense of his own power. He may be enraged, but his options remain good, and he can almost always find another woman to soothe his hurt. A woman whose man has left her is often totally on her own. Perhaps she can find another man to support her, perhaps not. If she has children, it's harder, of course, and she may have to go on welfare, move in with her parents, or sue for help through the courts. Men live in the external world; for them, women are recreation and the security in the home. For women outside the job market, home is their "work," and they have no recreation; even making love becomes one of their jobs. Men are their only source of security, and they must constantly be prepared to guard it, earn it, hold on to it. It is a sign of male chauvinism (men's constant putting down of women) that a man whose woman has left him usually insists that she has been "brainwashed"—he refuses to give her credit for making her own decisions, for controlling her own life. The frequent male paranoia about how *their* women are always apt to leave them for some stronger, more dashing man reflects male competitiveness, feelings of inadequacy, male's understanding of women as mindless chattel, and male use of women to bolster their own low self-esteem. Of course people are emotionally upset if their partner/mate leaves them; but this is not the issue here. What we are pointing out is that in terms of economic/social survival, women are more vulnerable in abandonment than men, whatever the psychological effects of such separation are for both.

Learning how to please men, women brutalize and humiliate themselves every day. Simone de Beauvoir's *The Second Sex* describes many of the growing-up feelings women have, and the male-created myths by which they must judge themselves.[4] In order to make men happy, women have to adopt attitudes that make them "weak" or "hysterical." Our culture demands that women behave passively and irrationally, and we then use such behavior as the "proof" that this is how women naturally are. Furthermore, women generally lead lives which produce in them the "hysterical" responses we expect: They are isolated, worked like slaves, treated like objects. Women who defy the stereotype are attacked both by women and men as "uppity" or "bitchy" or "unfeminine." A now famous study by Dr. Inge Broverman shows that the "ideal" man in this society has normal, healthy attributes; the "ideal" woman has attributes which define her as hysterical and unhealthy.[5] It becomes clear how cultural expectations create serious differences in behavior between the sexes, and perpetuate women's second-class status. The values, myths, and stereotypes in this political system are all male-created and male-serving. To succeed, women have to accept them and play by the rules. Thus they must degrade themselves and violate their integrity.

Juliet Mitchell has pointed out how women's condition is determined by their part in four processes: production (industrial), reproduction (biological), sexuality (with its dual standards), and socialization (of children).[6] In each of

[4]Simone de Beauvoir, *The Second Sex* (New York: Knopf, 1953).

[5]Inge K. Broverman, Donald M. Broverman, Frank E. Clarkson, Paul S. Rosenkrantz, Susan R. Vogel, "Sex Role Stereotypes and Clinical Judgments of Mental Health," *Journal of Consulting and Clinical Psychologists*, Vol. 34, 1970.

[6]Juliet Mitchell, "Women: The Longest Revolution," available from New England Free Press.

these areas, women are given thankless tasks whose accomplishment brings them lesser status than men. They are told they are too weak or too dumb for more important tasks or responsibilities. (In the last century, women were told they were not bright enough to be typists; when men became bored with that skill, women were quickly "promoted.") Men control production, regulate reproduction, promulgate the myths of sexuality, and dictate the correct ways of socialization. And they refuse to change women's position.

Challenging male control brings us into direct conflict with the status quo and with the political realities of this country. I saw women in the air force who were trapped in social expectations and custom; they did what they were supposed to do because if they objected they were ostracized and became objects of social cruelty, rumor, and backbiting. They were treated like property. I knew women who were kept in their own houses, forbidden to go shopping or to talk to anyone other than their husbands. One woman was not permitted to talk to other men, to drive a car, to work, or save money—all because her husband was fanatically afraid he would *lose her* if she so much as spoke to another man. Another woman's husband beat her regularly when he was drunk; because he was a good worker, he managed to keep the military bosses on his side, and her complaints went unheeded. She lived in daily terror of the man. Some women were frightened because they could not "really love" their husbands, and were afraid to admit their lack of sexual ardor. They felt sure that their husbands, oppressive and demanding for the most part, would become enraged at them. When some of these women spoke to lawyers, they were told to be quiet and accept it; "domestic squabbles" rarely seemed worthy of the law's gravity.

Over and over again, we have met a profound despair and frustration in women referred to us as "patients" because their perceptions were being denied and suppressed. Instead of being able to express their anger, they were forced to swallow it. They felt helpless, inadequate, responsible for their own misery, and accepted the situation as the best they might reasonably hope for. It is no wonder that more women than men are psychiatric patients. Many women's situations leave them few options other than chronic depression, pill taking, acting out, psychosomatic diseases, psychotherapy, or suicide.

Women, often outside the forces of production in this society, have less power in society than men. But in one area they do have the ability to crush and destroy—in their sexual relations. Sex is a weapon prepared for women by their oppressors. With it they can challenge men, trap them, retaliate against them; it gives them the power to create or destroy a man's self-esteem, even to destroy him sexually. But, when women feel forced to use sex for their own survival they engage in a form of prostitution. Sex as manipulation instead of an expression of feeling alienates women from their own minds and bodies, and objectifies them, i.e., makes them into sexual "objects."

The price of having such a weapon is high: Women become vulnerable to men's attraction to them. If they perform poorly, they can be ignored or replaced. Once they accept the rules of the game, they are judged by them too. Thus they are trapped in a losing duality. They begin to perceive themselves through men's eyes—as mindless bodies, sex objects, blank screens for fantasies to be projected on. The price of playing by the man's rules is a wretched schizophrenia between inner self (what's really me) and outer self (who I have to be for all those people out there). Gradually the inner self starts judging the woman by her outer self, the two become confused, and the mask of social convenience, which had been loosely worn and easily discarded, suddenly seems to be tightly stuck in a nightmarish way.

Women are thus damaged psychologically, politically, and socially by the sexist oppression which permeates this society. This fact needs to be kept in mind by anyone concerned with "therapy" and its role in dealing with "emotional problems."

Men, of course, are not oppressed in the same ways women are, but they are oppressed nonetheless—in terms of class, race, nationality, or self-relationship. In the ways that men oppress women, there may be an "oppression of the oppressors." We're not terribly concerned with that. We feel it's up to men to challenge their own oppression and get off women's backs. Only in this way will men be able to understand fully their own oppression and go on to revolutionary work. Men who cannot deal with their own sexism will have to deal with the consequences of their oppressiveness.

I can discuss the effects of sexism on men best by referring to my own experience. In our opinion, men profit from sexism in this society; but they are destroyed as human beings in the process. Men absorb sexist myths and values during all their formative years. They are kept from their feelings, forced into "masculine" molds just as surely as women are thrust into being "feminine," and deprived of their humanity. Though they gain in terms of privilege and power, they lose an awareness of themselves as people.

I know from my own experience that men don't stop sexist behavior until they are confronted with it, until they are frightened and challenged and are no longer in control. There is no motivation to change other than the imminent loss of privilege. Men are willing to take advantage of their position as long as they can get away with it, as long as they can avoid any struggle.

In my own case, for instance, it was only when my wife drew back from me, confronted me angrily, and announced she would no longer tolerate the old ways, that I had any reason to change. Even so, the process was difficult. The changes I was able to make opened my eyes to the effects of sexism on men and women and on male-female relationships.

Growing up a white man in America trained me to be an oppressor. Step by step, it damaged me psychologically, moved from one dehumanization process to the next. My middle-class position had a lot to do with this; I'm sure working-class men are taught other ways of oppressing women and one another. For me, success and failure were the major determinants of my worth, but success was defined in academic and affluent terms. I had to get good grades, had to look forward to college and a good job. Others I knew were taught to regard physical prowess as the crucial mark; they fought one another, engaged in sports, and later competed sexually with one another for various women. Being a person had little to do with anything. The world was reduced to things which could be won and possessed—people, cars, grades, women, friends.

I competed from the beginning. I followed academic interests with great energy and delighted in being on top of the class. Instead of using my mind to help my peer group, I used it to obtain a prominent position for myself. I had no understanding of how I cooperated in shaming my peers, in basing my "success" on their failure, in climbing over them intellectually just as they competed with one another through physical fights. Even at home, I competed with my sister and was too busy "doing things" to get close to her.

Deep down I felt inadequate and was afraid to let anyone know it. I was a year younger than the others in my class (the result of skipping a year to "get ahead"). I was shorter than the other guys, awkward and self-conscious. In the common bathroom I was very self-conscious about my body: I felt my penis was too short and was afraid of the actual *physicality* of the place, especially as most of my activity was mind-based. I could make up for my physical "flaws" by excelling in school; but all the while I sensed that other guys disliked me and I felt uneasy around them. Since I wasn't really sure of my intelligence —I thought it was probably pretense and acting—I was constantly afraid of revealing myself.

In the fourth grade, one of the girls and I showed our genitals to each other—in school. We were caught, and I was chastised for it. It affected my attitudes about sex and made it something private and naughty. It also made me feel that, deep down, I was "nasty" as well as inadequate.

By the time I reached adolescence, I was planning to go to college. I was competitive with others, frightened and fascinated by women, and very much engaged in sexual fantasies in which I was strong and assertive and imagined that women gave in and did whatever I commanded. Meanwhile, in real life, I was shy.

With all my performing, I was very caught up in activities and not as in touch with my own feelings as I could have been. Instead of sensing how afraid I was, I felt self-important. Whenever I became upset from some interpersonal slight, I could retreat into books or into my sexual fantasies. I thought that if I could become a Great Man, women would flock around me. I couldn't imagine that any woman would like me for myself, without all the honors and awards, without the drive and compulsion.

Sexuality, rather than bringing me more *into* the world, kept me from it. I was intensely involved with masturbation, sexual fantasies, and feelings of being sexually inadequate. Books and movies reinforced my view of sex as a wild domination/subjugation event, overlaid with all sorts of romantic mythology. All my fantasies involved my dominating women I'd seen casually, or women I wanted to speak to and date but was afraid of. In retrospect, I can understand these fantasies as restorative, as balancing the defects I felt I had. But they were exactly the fantasies that led me to sadistic manipulation of other people, to fear of and anger at women; these fantasies, so common in men, are the basis for sexist behavior in actuality.

In the absence of any genuine involvement, my fantasies mushroomed. I imagined—and this went on into college years and beyond—that I could find the Perfect Woman somewhere; she would make me into the Adequate Man. I would never have to struggle with her, fight with her, worry with her, because she would ideally take care of me, understand me, and satisfy all my needs and desires. Then I went into the world trying to match women against this monstrous image.

When I failed to find such a person, I imagined that (1) I was a creep and the Ideal Woman would not love me, and (2) all women were creeps except for this one Ideal Woman, who I'd have to spend my whole life looking for. In the meantime, I felt like a fool because my friends were much more successful with girls than I. I felt awkward and stiff, embarrassed at my body—my thick thighs, my adolescent fat, my pimples—and afraid that others would find me unattractive. I was so paralyzed by the fear of rejection that I never made a move. Even during junior year in France, in love with one of the girls on the trip, I was unable to make an advance toward her, afraid she'd put me off. The idea of failing seemed worse than not trying. By not trying, you can always preserve the illusion that you could have succeeded, if only you'd tried.

I grew up alienated from other men, whom I feared: I competed with them, felt their anger and resentment, envied and mistrusted them. I did not understand the working-class kids in my high school, and felt inferior to the preppies I encountered at Princeton; I felt intimidated by people who were physically stronger than I, yet not fully at home with intellectuals.

I was alienated also from women, whom I wished to control, whom I feared for their power to crush my self-esteem, and whom I mistrusted because of this fear. I saw them as sexual objects, thus trying to make them inferior by dehumanizing them. I could not treat women as people and thus could not be a man myself.

I couldn't develop love for men because I constantly feared and mistrusted them too. I couldn't express my love for women because I feared them and needed to control and neutralize them first. I couldn't love myself because I thought I was inadequate, worthless, and shabby. My only ways out of it all were to excel academically, to retreat into the world of fantasy—books, writing poems and plays, acting—and to treat all other people like things, thus making them controllable.

I couldn't afford to be close to anyone. I couldn't accept anyone as a close friend: women were likely to be stolen away—they were sexual objects; men couldn't be trusted —they were my competitors. Thus I had to dominate everyone, or feel dominated by them; there was no middle ground in my cosmos, and mutuality was unknown.

In the middle of an identity crisis during my first year in graduate school, I resolved to get myself a profession. At the same time I got married. Both acts were designed to give me some security at a time when my most profound insecurities were coming out. The profession I pursued led to its own contradictions. The marriage, which had come from a genuine feeling of love and affection, became harsh and cruel as I extracted emotional sustenance from my wife while at the same time insisting on my being in command. I insisted that she admire me as much as I wanted to admire myself; she had to follow my lead; she had to deny her own self in order to further my plans. When she finally understood how fundamentally undazzling I was, she was shocked and angry. She felt tricked and manipulated. And she was right. I, like many other men, had used her to be my security while I frolicked in the real world. At the same time I helped keep her from developing into what she was by keeping her subordinate.

I was unaware of what was going on, and I think she

was too, for a long time. All we knew was that there was an awful tension between us, a sense of not being together, a feeling of resentment and incompletion, bickering and arguing, childish games and rituals meant to cover up the lack of good feeling. There seemed to be no way out of it. Each squabble led to another; and the resolutions were never thorough. The inequality of power and privilege kept up and gnawed away at each of us.

She finally joined the women's movement, after she had built up a lot of anger and a vast distance had come between us. We still had tender feelings for each other, but they were buried beneath layers of frustration and bitterness. We built up many walls, many secrets, many feelings and acts we were afraid to share. We would not risk the openness which might have helped us until it was almost too late.

Our intimate life had become stereotyped and fantasy ridden. It was hard for us to have fun together, and being serious was deadly. When we finally confronted each other we were honest, but it was difficult to see how we'd be able to change things. Some things between us did become more natural, more accepting, once the myths were shattered, but the unequal power situation remained. The resentments over the past years, past secrets, past humiliations and disappointments remained and grew. We struggled for a time to change. In the end, though, changes came too fast and too furiously to be accepted and assimilated. She could not avoid hurting me deeply in order to become the person she was, *her own* person; and I could not avoid hurting her deeply in order to get away from my own pain. Finally, we separated. What we learned through the suffering will, I hope, help us both avoid making these mistakes again.

I can still feel the sexist voice inside my head. I know what it says, and I recognize it as the voice of my adolescent peers chortling over how much of a girl's body they managed to feel before the evening's date was through.

It talks about women as sex objects, feels that sex is everything, wants men to be strong and in control, insists that it's weak to show feelings, feels contemptuous of gay people, trusts no one, and feels constantly afraid that others will take its possessions. The only way to combat that kind of thinking is to identify it, analyze its roots, and challenge it.

I can understand men feeling that their whole security depends on the women they *control,* on the women they possess like so many cattle. Their self-esteem is wholly dependent on this. Wilhelm Reich[7] has focused on this phenomenon—the authoritarianism of the nuclear family, the tyranny of sexual repression and fantasies which make women and men into objects. That's the way all of us grew up in this country.

We can't change this until we change the whole society. It won't "just happen." Attitudes won't change until the institutions that build the attitudes change. This is why defeating sexism must be part of a revolutionary struggle, and why it will not come about until political power changes hands and institutions stop serving the people they now serve. This is why it is important to understand how each institution in this society—schools, therapy, jobs, media—oppresses us by foisting racist, sexist, imperialist practice on us.

Every institution in a sexist society is marked by sexism. Psychotherapy, far from being an exception, is one of the best examples of this.

Most therapists are men; most patients women. Many female therapists, trying to make it in a male world, accept the predominant (male) notions in their field; they act as oppressively toward women as do their male colleagues. Think, for example, of Helene Deutsch and

[7]Wilhelm Reich, *The Mass Psychology of Fascism* (New York: Farrar, Straus & Giroux, 1971).

Myrnia Farnham, whose Freudian apologies in the 1940s and 1950s told women to accept anatomy as their destiny, to go back to the kitchen and bedroom and playroom, and to learn to fulfill themselves in this way. After all, babies are women's way of finally getting a substitute penis.

The traditional psychological notions of women—all written by men—set the groundwork for therapists treating women as inferiors. Women are supposed to be weak, hysterical, silly, immature, sexual/fecund/maternal. Maladaptive creatures, their role in life is to bear children and serve their men. If they want to do something "on their own," it has to be during their time off. If they devote full time to their own lives, they are called selfish, masculine, and aggressive/striving/neurotic. These myths have been challenged only recently, but not, of course, destroyed. The therapy world eagerly makes one or two concessions (wiping out the notion of penis envy, for example). But the basic power difference is maintained—that is, women must yearn for subordinate relationships with men, for marriage, and for children.

Women patients receive slipshod care—unless they happen to be young, bright, verbal, and not all that sick, in which case they may find some young therapist who is eager to spend "professional" time with them. Married women get medications and advice when they are angry and depressed, group therapy to make their marriages click, the latest advice on making themselves sexually attractive, or hormones to make their skin and tempers sleeker. When they finally fall into catatonic or profoundly depressive states, or when they slide out of touch with their oppression into some realm of tortured fantasy, they are apt to be committed by some "concerned" relative—an angry husband or frustrated parents—and receive a "curative" course of half a dozen or more electroshock treatments to bring them back to the "real world." Older women and poor women, women who are dowdy and women who speak little English—all receive the standard drugs and quickie (short-term) therapy. The state hospitals are filled with lower-class women who have been driven mad and abandoned, and whose custodial care is now left to the mental health people. We have seen, in a community psychiatric service in New York's Washington Heights, how older, Spanish-speaking, and black women are shuttled to state hospitals or drug-treatment units, while the cute young girls—so challenging and seductive—become the male residents' "long-term treatment cases." (It's not clear which is a worse fate.)

Therapists go along with attacking "uppity" women who challenge social customs. If they irritate or push the therapist, he will reach into his arsenal of terms and denounce them as castrating and neurotic, as people with "sexual confusion," poor "identifications," "ego-lacunae," "borderline personalities," and so on. Diagnoses are political statements, and women are labeled again and again for unfeminine behavior.

Some therapists exploit women by playing with their minds; others by playing with their bodies. (A panel at the 1971 annual meeting of the Association for Humanist Psychology discussed whether a therapist should go to bed with his/her patient if mutually attracted; the patients were, of course, women, the therapists, men.) We're not attacking the idea that people who help each other might also make love together; what we *are* attacking is the unchecked, arrogant use of women patients by male therapists as outlets for their own sex and power fantasies. The oppressive way therapy is used makes us want to support a current puritanical standard as almost the only guarantee of a therapist's nonexploitativeness. In the future, when therapy is a different kind of institution, intimacy between therapist and client may be a different matter.

Therapists who sexually "exploit" their patients usually rationalize (mystify) it by the most elegant professional-sounding talk. This kind of sexual "liberation" has to be called what it really is: exploitation of women's minds and bodies by pig therapists. The encounter movement too has exploited women in this way. Lovemaking, after all, *can* and *should* be loving and supportive, but it can also be cruelly exploitative. The quality depends on the context and on the power distribution.

Therapists attempt to brainwash women just as they try to brainwash gays, the young, radicals, and any others who defy today's oppressive social laws. They deny their patients' perceptions, telling a woman she isn't really angry at her husband, but at the boredom of her life. They encourage her to develop a hobby. They tell patients they "really feel" something they don't feel. They tell a woman she "really feels" inadequate and dependent on her husband, instead of angry and resentful; or that her sense of inadequacy is *really* responsible for her anger. They urge their patients to adjust to the "reality" of their lives. They encourage a woman to use Valium or Librium to help her get through her household chores instead of encouraging her to challenge her husband about the division of household labor, or to get a part-time job and force her husband to share the housework, or to reexamine if indeed she really wants to stay in the home situation and, if not, what options she has. Therapists, themselves married, liberal or otherwise, working while their wives stay home with the kids (or, even more chic, have a job themselves while a maid takes care of the house and/or children), tell women that their role is to have children, to enjoy sex with their boy friends or husbands, and to be happy partners. Therapists rarely challenge their own middle-class bias, their own nuclear-family orientation. They see gay women and gay men as sick. They use their power to gain selfish, unfeeling ends: denying women abortions in situations where psychiatric opinions are essential for gaining permission; encouraging them to stay in messy family situations, where their husbands beat them or keep them virtually chained to the house; telling women who have sexual difficulties to "loosen up," without investigating the context in which their resentment and lack of sexual responsiveness might be entirely justified; and so on. And all the time, the therapists are getting wealthy by seeing these women as patients.

Therapists don't arrive innocently at society's stereotypes of women. They helped make these stereotypes themselves, and they help push them, as gospel, on the public. The notion that women are naturally passive and not aggressive, that women have a parental instinct (but men don't), that women are naturally more emotional than men, are mythical creations of therapists in this society. These men do not understand women's experience; they deride women's consciousness and refuse to adapt their theories to the facts. By perpetuating the division of power through sex, they contribute to women's oppression; by "treating" them, they act as a fifth-column group of even more subtle oppressors: pigs in sheep's clothing.

Women must be wary of male therapists.

Any woman in therapy should be in a women's liberation or consciousness-raising group at the same time; perhaps she should only be in a C-R group, and not in therapy at all. She should certainly be talked to clearly by her therapist, who should make cos own bias clear to her and say how co stands regarding women's liberation issues, sexuality, monogamy, gay relationships, marriage, child rearing, and the relationship of men to women. She can then decide whether she can trust co enough to work openly with co. If not, she should never, never be coerced —by guilt, shame, pressure—into staying with co in therapy.

Why am I so certain about this? Because I have seen it happen with myself. I have oppressed women who were my patients, and I have seen many, many other women oppressed in the same way.

84

Let me talk plainly about how male therapists have oppressed women patients, about how even female therapists have put women down. It happens every day, in every hospital, every clinic, every private office, every teaching center, every city, every state, everywhere.

I have seen a couple with marital difficulties and have —as the therapist—snickered with the husband who is mocking his wife's situation while she struggled with our mutually piggish behavior, trying to explain why she felt hopeless and depressed. Instead of asking him why he found her anger and despair so humorous—his snicker implied that the "little woman" really took things much too seriously, almost to the point of being comical—I nodded and smiled at his invitation of support, just as I had been programmed to do all my life. I responded to the fraternal friendship and let her torment go unrecognized.

I have encouraged women patients to play sexy games with me. I have looked at their legs and admired their breasts. I'm sure they felt this "interest" on my part; and those who needed to "please me" did so by dressing even more seductively, by wiggling around, and putting on a show. (I have seen research films about psychotherapy sessions that clearly show the body movements of male therapist and female client to be symmetrical, perfectly timed, and extremely sexual, like a bird's mating dance. With male patients, male therapists tend to align themselves much more toward outright dominance/submission issues.) I've thus encouraged women to placate and please me with their bodies, and have gotten my jollies off them in therapy sessions when I was supposed to be helping them with their problems.

I have talked to long-term, "intensive psychotherapy" patients in depth about their feelings for me, about their dreams which I interpreted as being about me, about their fantasies of seducing me or living with me. I have acted to increase their fantasies about me, which I then analyzed. The result of this has been to confuse women, to put them down, to feel my own ego swell because of their affection, and to manipulate them for my own ends. I had fantasies of making love to various women, which I hid from them—fantasies which, if we'd been in a different power/social context, might have been reasonable, but which, in this particular situation, were power-hungry fantasies, undisclosed, parasitic, oppressive. I can easily understand therapists manipulating women into wanting to have sex with them. It has happened to me too, and I usually implied that such a feeling on a patient's part was part of *her* "pathology," *her* problem, *her* inability to accept the unreality of the not quite real therapy situation. This way the therapist gets his cake and eats it too—by making the patient responsible for *his* own fantasies.

At times when I felt inadequate and lonely, I tried to bolster my self-esteem by impressing women patients with my skill in interpreting dreams, or with my humanity or my style, not by helping them with their problems.

In therapy, the therapist has a dozen possible leads to follow. What makes him pursue one line rather than another? When a patient related a dream, what made me seek to find myself in it rather than to understand its value for her? When a patient related an experience about a date, what made me seek out the juicier details rather than the simple political/personal facts of the experience? I think the answers lie in the reasons why people become therapists and how they use their power as therapists.

I have gone along with self-destructive behavior by my women patients—one whose whole life centered around the fantasy of trapping a Worthwhile Man, for whom she would always be willing to immolate herself; another whose guilt about an abortion totally invalidated her sense of self and who could not begin to think of herself as a good human being; another who was gay and whom I encouraged to explore the straight part of herself at a time when such exploration was totally at odds with her life; one striving, capable woman whom I kept jabbing at, teasing, kidding, to pick away at her self-esteem, until she finally "admitted" that deep down she felt inadequate (which made me superior); one young girl whom I encouraged to go out on dates and to stay in school so she'd be less crazy; one Puerto Rican teenager whom I encouraged to challenge her father's authority when it was clear that her father would not tolerate such a challenge and that I wouldn't back her up. So she got a beating and I got nothing.

I have sympathized with shy, twitchy male patients who felt inadequate and encouraged them in behavior which treated women as objects to be exploited and used, not as people. I'd encourage them to find a woman so as to feel more of a man. I agreed with them in their view of sex and sexual performance and dominance as a sign of manhood. I have let obvious chauvinistic rationalization pass without pointing it out because I'd wanted to maintain my patient's good will, because of the money he was paying me, and because I didn't disagree all that much with him to begin with.

I have believed that some women patients felt "weak" because they were women and had not known a good man who could "turn them on," and that what they needed was a warm and loving man, a good sex life, and attention. I kept counseling one woman to go places where she could find such a man. I commiserated with her disappointing forays, but never questioned why she should think only about "a good catch." For a time I viewed one woman as masochistic and unable to change her living situation, but once I had confronted her with my feelings, she was able to act strongly and confront her husband and eventually leave him.

I have counseled women who were married and had

children, and did not understand the oppressive routine of their daily lives. Instead I talked about their expressing their anger, urged them to come to terms with their minds, their dreams, their family histories, instead of challenging the way things are.

I have kidded and disparaged women co-workers, taking liberties with them I never took with men, resorting to sexual innuendo to put down social workers in the institution where I trained, cavalierly treating their ideas: I was certain *I* knew what was best and that they had better be helpful and subordinate.

I have been annoyed by quarrelsome, depressed women, and given them tranquilizers, antidepressants, sleeping pills, anything to get them off my back—at the same time fostering the mystique of being a therapist. Rather than express my despair at their routinized, depersonalized lives, I tolerated their complaining and simply medicated them when they became too burdensome. Menopausal women have made me headachy and angry; trying to get long-suffering housewives who came for treatment of well-justified phobic symptoms to change their behavior drove me crazy when, instead, I could have commiserated with their situation and explored with them just why it was so inviting, yet threatening to emerge into the outside world.

I have lied to women about my own feelings toward them, denying that I was angry or bored or attracted, thus contributing to their feeling crazy. One woman used to get on my nerves because she was always demanding that I do something for her, that I be Supershrink. I was angry; she picked up on it. Rather than discuss with her why she felt that I could straighten out her life for her, and examine the role she put me in and the basis for her getting angry at my own willingness to play that role, I kept my anger to myself, feeling—in a condescending way—that if I was honest about my feelings she'd collapse and I wouldn't be able to help her. Finally I did admit my anger. We got along much better and more honestly.

All this goes beyond therapy. I, like other therapists, have treated women in my life as if they were patients too, as if their duty was to serve me, to be my security, to boost my self-esteem.

But it also goes beyond a matter of personal politics. It reflects the same experience other men live, over and over, relationship after relationship. It reflects the way of looking at women as sex objects, as things to be handled and conquered. It reflects the attitude of not quite taking women, their lives, or their complaints seriously. It reflects the attitude that allows men almost any license with their wives and children short of overt violence and degradation.

We cannot minimize the noxious effects of sexist therapy on women. We know what we have done. We know what others have done too—teachers leering at women's legs and breasts, colleagues making obscene jokes at women's expense, friends being obsessed with sex and treating all their women patients as objects for their own amusement, encounter-group leaders exploiting their power by bandying women about sexually and emotionally.

Therapists are under no scrutiny. They operate behind closed doors. They run clinics which are not publicly accountable, commit people to hospitals against their will, overprescribe drugs. Such power is corrupting and, in the end, destructive. But this should be no surprise: It follows inevitably from therapy's function in a sick, capitalist society. How could we expect it to be otherwise?

6

Sexuality and Sensuality

In our consumer society, sex is both a commodity and an advertising gimmick. Sexuality thus becomes distorted, sexual communication and sensual enjoyment become blocked or cut off from other aspects of relationships, and various other activities are turned to for some kind of sexual thrill. We are obsessed with sex. Those who insist on strict monogamy, chastity before marriage, and the like, are just as symptomatic of the mania as those who throw themselves into compulsory promiscuity, who regard sexual intercourse as equivalent to brushing one's teeth, and who denounce love and fidelity as bourgeois attitudes.

It's impossible to travel around this country without being barraged by sexual stimuli. People's clothing is suggestive: bras and no bras, short skirts, tight pants, skimpy shorts, exaggerated ways of carrying oneself. Countless billboards, TV programs, ads, magazines, movies, jokes, books, condition us to expect sexual thrills from one another and from commodities we consume. Popular songs echo and reinforce this expectation. Over and over, our training makes us regard one another as sexual machines. Sex becomes at the same time much more and much less than it really is.

Women are reinforced daily to believe that their role

is to be bodies on display; men are kept in a state of constant sexual readiness, titillated and leering. Actual relationships become blunted and narrowed. Our feelings parody TV serials and ads. Life mimics pop art.

We develop a mystique about sex, emphasizing how conquest and performance are essential: Sex becomes a way of manipulating or obtaining power. Men measure their worth by the number of women they can "lay," by the resourcefulness of their lovemaking techniques. Women measure their worth by the number of men they can "trap," by the excitement they can produce or the desire they can incite. Thus follow the hundreds of consumer products aimed at increasing or lubricating sexual performance: cars, groovy clothes, flashy apartment interiors, stereo sets, records, electric razors, strawberry douches, shiny lipsticks, body creams, deodorants, and so forth. Having a partner gives us status; having none takes it away.

Beneath this is the profound insecurity and fear we all develop as we grow up being treated like things, not people. Alienated from our own bodies, we surrender to the allure of ads and fantasy. We believe that pleasure and self-esteem can be bought with enough dollars, pretense, and conquest. We cut ourselves off from one another and try desperately to insure survival and security by manipulating others. Fear gnaws at us and makes any real commitment to another impossible. Thus we indulge in game playing and pseudointimacy, and genuine intimacy, which we all crave, eludes us. We settle for an imitation because the real thing threatens us too much.

Sex in the United States has become a duty. Husbands have a duty to give their wives orgasms, and wives have a duty to give their husbands sexual pleasure and release; everyone has a right to give herself/himself pleasure. Partners have a duty to find the correct techniques. "Movement" people have a duty to experiment with multirelationships, gay relationships, and so forth. No matter what your orientation, there's a concomitant duty toward sexual experience. Chaste or promiscuous, it is still our *duty*, still part of our obsession with sex.

On the surface we appear to be secure and self-reliant; deeper down we are frightened and insecure. Many of us keep moving so fast we fail to see what it is we really feel. When we do manage to glimpse that level we get scared away, sensing that we are really empty or meaningless. Thus we rarely manage to experience the emptiness which is rightfully ours, nor the even deeper sense of solidity—the sense of existing in this world, accepting its limitations and reality, and enduring.

SEXUALITY BETWEEN MEN AND WOMEN

Relationships between men and women tend to focus around issues of dominance and submission, so it's natural that sexuality becomes similarly polarized. "Free" or "spontaneous" sexuality is rare—both in long-lasting relationships and in brief, fleeting ones. Sexual conquest becomes a way of establishing power, of gaining strength through another's submission of gaining security through acquiescence to a stronger person's will. (Similar aspects of sexual relationships exist, of course, between homosexuals too.)

Sex thus means defeating or performing, not getting close. Orgasm is burdened by its being a "surrender" and therefore a desired power commodity. Pleasure winds up in second place.

Because sex is made into an object, women and men manage to dehumanize one another as they pursue sexual success. Treating the other as an object, they feel themselves treated as objects too. Women grow up constantly feeling themselves "objectified" by men. They are seen as a collection of a smile, two breasts, an ass, two legs, and so on. The person who possesses these parts is ignored by the "appreciative" males, though. Many women are made to resent their own bodies, and they become alienated from and disgusted with themselves: Menstruation become repulsive, body hair offensive. The taboo against the physical body goes with our idealization of cleanliness and horror of dirt.

Men feel uneasy in their bodies too, sensing that women are judging them by their height, muscles, erections. Sexism comes full circle as women apply men's own distorted concerns back on them.

When people treat one another as objects, the natural response is to feel estranged and then angry. Much tension between couples stems from each using the other as a thing. A wife who does not experience orgasm may be furious at her husband's treating her as a receptacle; her anger is justified. A man's trouble with his erection may be related to his self-esteem, to the use of sex as power. Angry arguments over who is meeting whose needs also often reflect the partners' irrational demands for power over the other.

Herbert Marcuse has introduced the notion of *repressive desublimation*[1] to deal with the new, seemingly permissive sexual practices. Sex attitudes and practices appear liberalized, whereas in reality they mask a strict binding to cultural values—objectification of sex, consumerism, and so on. They manage to preserve a repressive outlook while opening up the range of pleasures. Again, the pleasures become compulsory. The very ways we pursue pleasure are dictated to us.

Marcuse's argument is that sexuality has become more and more available, but in the service of containing peo-

[1]Herbert Marcuse, *Eros and Civilization* (Boston: Beacon Press, 1955); *An Essay on Liberation* (Boston: Beacon Press, 1969).

ple's sexuality and making them more manageable through social control.

It has often been noted that advanced industrial civilization operates with a greater degree of sexual freedom—"operates" in the sense that the latter becomes a market value and a factor of social mores. Without ceasing to be an instrument of labor, the body is allowed to exhibit its sexual features in the everyday work world and in work relations. This is one of the unique achievements of industrial society—rendered possible by the reduction of dirty and heavy physical labor; by the availability of cheap, attractive clothing, beauty culture, and physical hygiene; by the requirements of the advertising industry, etc. . . .

This socialization is not contradictory but complementary to the de-eroticization of the environment. Sex is integrated into work and public relations and is thus made more susceptible to (controlled) satisfaction. . . .

The range of socially permissible and desirable satisfaction is greatly enlarged, but through this satisfaction, the Pleasure Principle is reduced—deprived of the claims which are irreconcilable with the established society. Pleasure, thus adjusted, generates submission. . . .

In light of the cognitive function of this mode of sublimation, the desublimation rampant in advanced industrial society reveals its truly conformist function. This liberation of sexuality (and of aggressiveness) frees the instinctual drives from much of the unhappiness and discontent that elucidate the repressive power of the established universe of satisfaction. To be sure, there is pervasive unhappiness, and the happy consciousness is shaky enough—a thin surface over fear, frustration and disgust. This unhappiness leads itself easily to political mobilization; without room for conscious development, it may become the instinctual reservoir for a new fascist way of life and death. But there are many ways in which the unhappiness beneath the happy consciousness may be turned into a source of strength and cohesion for the social order.[2]

Thus the new permissiveness threatens no one. It unleashes and satisfies certain sex/power drives, but it does not begin to challenge social norms. Consumption of goods goes on; nuclear families continue. If anything changes, it is the appetite for more of the groovy, titillating stuff now permitted. A generation of people live out the fantasies that society's repression had forbidden. We should not only stop the way society represses and then, under strict control, permits exploration, but also challenge the very patterns of education and growth. But this, of course, is not permitted.

GENITALITY

One heritage from Freud is the view that the "mature" individual is one who has maintained or obtained a "genital-sexual orientation." The stages of human sexual development are seen as oral/anal/phallic/genital; people with problems are stuck (regressed, fixated) at some earlier level. The implications of this framework range from "what she needs is a good fuck" to "make love not war," with a whole landscape in between. The genital-primacy view holds, for instance, that sex play is appropriate only if it "leads" to genital intercourse. Genital intercourse becomes the norm. Other forms of sex play, if indulged in "too much," constitute a "perversion."

The genital-primacy view also condemns homosexuality as a perversion resulting from an "arrested" development. Strong emotions—disgust, condemnation—become glued to certain kinds of sexuality—oral-genital

[2]Herbert Marcuse, *One-Dimensional Man* (Boston: Beacon Press, 1964), pp. 74–75.

relations, ano-genital relations, homosexual relations. Where do these emotions come from? From the culturally determined notions of normality and from this society's abhorrence of "abnormality," which is believed sick, dangerous, and disturbed. Therapists have been quick to describe certain sexual customs as abnormal and thus to develop and bolster the notion of genital primacy.

A few things about sex should be evident to anyone who reflects on cos own experience. Genitals themselves don't care who fondles them; the mind may worry about what's happening, but the organ responds to touch in the same way every time, if we let it. The entire body— breasts, lips, anus, genitals, neck, ears, armpits, wrists, toes—is capable of responding warmly to caresses. It is only our heads that tell us not to respond, that make us uptight, that encourage us to feel embarrassed, threatened, not quite right. We say "no" with our heads, not with our bodies.

What this means is that the talk about genital primacy doesn't make sense. People's bodies are responsive, and that is all. The patterns of sexual fondling are culturally determined: Certain things are taboo, and others are encouraged.

Masturbation too is natural. If we cannot love ourselves, as David Cooper points out in *The Death of the Family*, then we cannot love another either.[3] Experiences with alcohol or marijuana or with stronger drugs show us that, with our inhibitions out of the way and our receptivity turned up, we can find sensual stimulation and absolute pleasure in a great variety of body ways. One conclusion might be that touching our own and one another's bodies is OK if there is no exploitation going on —that is, if both people agree freely to what is happening. If we are loving and respectful of one another, if we inflict

[3]David Cooper, *The Death of the Family* (New York: Pantheon, 1970), pp. 41–42.

no pain and do not objectify the other or ourselves, then sensuality has a chance of opening up. The anxiety, guilt, and inhibition expressed by our permissive society is incredible.

We must underline how difficult it is to attain a free and wholesome sexuality in our competitive, capitalist society. Relationships between equals can be rewarding and beautiful, but our society makes it difficult—if not impossible—for lovers to be equals. Fellatio, for instance, can be a loving act between two people, but in a society in which sex is power and sucking someone off is a sign of submission, it's very hard to have this simple sensual experience. The prerequisite for an open sensuality seems to be trust stemming from a sense of self-adequacy and self-worth.

The obsession with genital sex produces all sorts of problems. It is responsible for the husband who tries relentlessly to bring his wife to orgasm—to "prove" that he is himself worthwhile. It is responsible for the mystique of "how many times you came last night." It is responsible for the lack of loving foreplay which is, after all, only a prelude to the Ultimate Orgasm. It is responsible for the overvaluation of some parts of the body and the total avoidance of others. The obsession with "mature" genitality means that a vast potential in our sensual lives is hidden—the world of smells, tastes, touch, and glances all becomes secondary to the concern with genital pleasure and power. No wonder we're constantly exposed to new products which desexualize our bodies—remove our hair, abolish our odors, cleanse offensive tastes. Nothing is left but the Big Genital Payoff, neutralized and hygienic. In the name of sex, we have destroyed sensuality, abolished ecstasy, and made pleasure a duty. No wonder people are upset by those who look hairy, who have body odors, who announce they are gay, who are prepared to combat the dictum that coming is everything. This is the potential of the sexual liberation movement, but today it is a potential used to advance capitalism by selling more and more antisex products, not to free our lives for a more honest sexuality.

One of the gay movement's gifts to us all has been a critical reappraisal of sensual pleasure and an appreciation of sensuality beyond genital sex (which, for many people, is directly linked to the experience of oppression). Sue Katz has discussed this in "Some Thoughts after a Gay Women's Lib Meeting":

Physical contact and feeling have taken a new liberatory form. And we call that *Sensuality*. The women's movement in general, especially at the beginning, and gay feminism now is a fantastically sensual experience for me. I love my body and the bodies of my sisters. Physicality is now a creative non-institutionalized experience. It is touching and rubbing and cuddling and fondness. It is holding and rocking and kissing and licking. Its only goal is closeness and pleasure. It does not exist for the Big Orgasm. It exists for feeling nice. . . . If it does include genital experience, that may or may not be the beginning or the ending of the experience. It may be anywhere, or nowhere. . . . We are free to act without pressure. I refuse to feel like I must make a decision about whether to "put out" or not. There is no such thing as putting out among us. There is no set physical goal to our sensuality. There is no sex.

The whole language is oppressive. It is white, male-oriented and a way of being physical that can only draw up bad memories for a lot of us. . . . Having sex means accepting a set of criteria for "success." [This holds for most men now too.—MG]

Sensuality is formless and amorphous. It can grow and expand as we feel it. It is shared by everyone involved. It isn't something one puts out for another. . . . Sensuality is something that can be very collective. Sex is private and tense. Sensuality is something you want your best friends to feel and act on with your other best friends. Sex is something you want power and territorial rights over. Sex is localized in the pants and limited by that. Sensuality is all over and grows always . . . [4]

This kind of natural appreciation of sex, freed from the compulsion to be "hip," contrasts sharply with the consumerist sexuality found and encouraged in this country.

Sensual pleasure in a nonthreatening, accepting relationship fights against the repression we're all taught. Celebrating our own bodies undermines the tendency to objectify them. Whether through dance, movement, touching, licking, rubbing, hugging, whispering, nuzzling, fucking, whatever—we are able to reexperience ourselves as full, spontaneous people. This kind of sensuality is correctly seen as subversive by the ruling class, and it tries to bring sex under control again, in carefully regulating the way in which it is permitted, in structuring Esalen-type workshops where celebration of the body takes place in a reactionary political context (sexist, elitist, consumerist), and in making sexual permissiveness a new way of using people as sex objects.

We must be careful, though, not to treat sexuality apart from its social context. People who make a fetish of their "free" sensuality are likely to fall into individualism and self-indulgence. This is not liberation, and it will separate these people from the large majority of working people in this country.

SEXUAL LIBERATION

The new sexual permissiveness has been deceptive in several ways: (1) It cloaks the unquestioned puritanism of

[4]Sue Katz, *Radical Therapist*, 2 (1971):1.

most American homes; (2) it encourages sexist and dehumanizing practices; (3) it pretends that being allowed to have varied experiences, perhaps living out one's fantasies, is proof that the American way of life is getting more and more benevolent; and (4) it disguises the fact that sexual permissiveness is mostly a middle-class and youth-oriented phenomenon.

Playboy and *Cosmopolitan* sell the idea that sex is a thing to be bought and savored. People are objects to be seduced and enjoyed, and moral compunctions about sex are "old-fashioned." In this respect, the sexual permissiveness echoes recent attitudes of the left, which proclaim that love and fidelity are bourgeois traits and that people should be free to have sex with whomever they want, men or women, and that not doing this is equivalent to maintaining old "retrograde" attitudes.[5]

The dichotomy between real sexual *repression*—the rigidity of most people's sex lives and practices—and the sexual *license* purveyed by the media helps contribute to people's sense of inadequacy and frustration, and to their building fantasies about how they'll eventually be able to get what everyone else has. This may mean fantasizing about The Right Person; usually it means fantasizing about achieving success so that others will then be attracted to you and will be more easily manipulative for sex/power reasons.[6]

Some people seem to regard promiscuity in all its forms as sexual liberation. To us, this merely reflects an obsession with sex. Sexual liberation doesn't mean compulsive

[5]In this connection, Reimut Reiche's comments on the failure of the First Commune in Germany, which tried to fuse sexual liberation with communist politics, are enlightening. See his *Sexuality and Class Struggle* (New York: Pantheon, 1971).

[6]Papers by MIT undergraduates about sexual ambitions and sexual feelings show a quite regular male sense that social success will be correlated with sexual rewards. This is the system's use of sex to give its loyal workers further incentive and satisfaction.

sexuality: swinging, Don Juanism, prostituting oneself. Rather, it means accepting our natural sensuality in all its forms and accepting the fact that some people may want monogamous, some polygamous, and some no sexual relationships. The right to say *no* is crucial in a liberated zone.

Sexual liberation also means freedom from old sex-role stereotypes: men who can be gentle and loving, passive if they want; women who can be strong and resourceful, assertive and bright. Men who can be house-husbands, women who take a job and are out of the house. Much of this also revolves around community day-care programs and around ways of living collectively instead of only in nuclear families..

"Swinging," for example, is not sexual liberation and should not be mistaken for it. Swinging is a way of preserving the nuclear family and bourgeois marriage. So are all the permissive/accepting techniques in the popular book *Open Marriage*.[7] Basically, the attitude which supports swinging is that marriage is usually boring but useful, so why not keep people in marriage by letting them have sex with others without threatening the institution itself. Mistaking sexual frustration for the essential boring quality of marriage, people then go off to bed with their neighbors. All too often, though, such encounters are sterile and rigid. Studies of swingers themselves show a remarkable degree of banality and conventionality: dull houses, dull minds, dull lives. The cure doesn't fit the disease. Neither the swingers nor the open-marriage people seriously question the institution of marriage and the nuclear family, or examine its effects on people living in them. Repressive sexuality *furthers* the nuclear family and compulsory marriage. Attempts to "liberalize" the bondage are phony. Sexual performance remains blown way out of focus; male chauvinism is unquestioned; the

[7]Nena and George O'Neill, *Open Marriage: A New Life Style for Couples* (New York: Evans, 1972).

swingers seem bored, sad people whose values are materialistic and superficial.

There's a big difference between liberated sex practices and the new permissiveness. Pornography, see-through blouses, playboy pads, and wife swapping are part of a decadent search for new kicks—further slavery to the sexist ways of thinking about people. The permissiveness distributes "bread and circuses" to bored people, in hopes that they'll keep the economy going: more cars for status, more clothes for appearance, more cosmetics, more TV sets, and so on. People keep on working in and supporting the status quo. Unfortunately, the misery of their personal lives is directly related to the *alienation* their jobs and culture produce.

Sexual liberation, carried out through individualistic practices, will be unsuccessful. Self-indulgence is a reactionary stance.

SEXUAL LIBERATION AND CLASS PRIVILEGE

One aspect of the American obsession with sex is clear: It reflects a supposedly affluent life style in which people have leisure time to worry about sex, and into which massive amounts of money are poured to persuade people to buy sex-linked consumer products. Its orientation is middle class.

People in our society who don't have the money or time to while away must nonetheless face the sexual advertising which surrounds them. Thus we can find sex used to combat boredom and to bolster self-esteem in all classes. Workers without much leisure use casual sex as a way of relieving tension. While affluent young bachelors set up "sexy" apartments, working-class kids buy *Playboy* magazine or pornography and fantasize about sexual conquests. Working-class women spend money on cosmetics to catch the right guy. No one is free from the use of sex as a come-on for the American way of life. It is an expression of bourgeois ideology which, affecting us all, makes us competitive, isolated, and vulnerable.

Our cultural concern with sex as a commodity has several implications. It suggests that, in a world context, Americans may find themselves isolated by this concern and may have to struggle to get a broader perspective on the issue. This would hold for both the "mainstream" of sexual liberation/permissiveness—popular magazines, Esalen-type therapy, and so forth—and for the liberation movements which focus on sexuality—the gay movement, the women's movement.

Poorer countries in the midst of their revolutionary struggles don't have the leisure of affluence to worry about who sleeps with whom and how. Third world peoples are concerned with the life and death issues of fighting oppression (domestic/imperial), controlling their lives, having food to eat and homes to live in, controlling their means of production. In the United States too, many oppressed people are focused more on bread-and-butter struggles than on issues of sexuality, although this remains an important and relevant issue for them. Working-class black women can relate to issues of control of their own lives and freedom for relationships with others. Issues of male chauvinism and the relationship of the gay world to the revolutionary struggle are important in the urban centers of the United States where the gay population is considerable.

The point is not to get so mired in discussions of sexuality that the political struggle gets obscured. This has been a problem for many of the New Left groups concerned with sexuality: How much energy to devote to the issue? How widely to relate it to other concerns?

For example, it is one thing for the gay women's movement to raise the issue of sexuality, to discuss the politics of heterosexual domination, and to affirm the validity and strength of gay relationships, it is another to demand that all women be gay and to denounce any woman who has a relationship with a man. Similarly, it is one thing to demand that gay people have control over their own lives, and quite another to devote all one's energy to combating homosexual oppression without relating it to the wider political context. This whole debate over "bedroom politics" has split many groups and many friendships in the movement.

Issues of sexuality must be relevant, concrete, and particular. It is important to know which kinds of sexism oppress which people. Some issues are relevant to middle-class women, others to working-class women. Some people can take risks more easily than others, enjoy more privilege in their day-to-day lives than others.

Cultural imperialism can also emerge in this context. Our perspective on sexuality is based on our experiences in an imperialist country; we don't necessarily know what is best for other countries. Thus, to condemn Cuba's stand on homosexuality, or to bewail China's acceptance of the nuclear family may be inappropriate. We have to struggle within our own context.

We must be careful not to lay trips on sisters and brothers whose own life experiences differ from our own—specifically, to make demands that people loosen up their sexual relationships, that monogamy be smashed, that people stop living in nuclear families. For some people, these institutions may represent the only real security and protection they can find. One doesn't ask people in shaky situations to let go of the life jacket.

THERAPY AND GAY LIBERATION

The movement for gay liberation has grown over the past few years. By this time its gamut is wide, embracing people whose concerns range from practicing total political revolution to seeking greater tolerance and legal equality for gay people. To understand these issues in depth, the reader is referred to a number of excellent gay periodicals—*Come Out!, Kaleidoscope, Ain't I a Woman,* the *Detroit Gay Liberator, The Ladder, Fag Rag, Brother* —and to the many gay women's writings which are found in the women's liberation movement journals and books. Our concern with the movement is to discuss its contributions to our understanding of sexuality and to underline the ways therapy has contributed to the oppression of gay people in this country.

From Freud onward, therapists have viewed homosexuality as a sickness and perversion. Though he began with an attitude of innate bisexuality, Freud moved later to consider the homosexual as fixated at a certain immature stage of development. This psychological view of gay people as "sick" fits the social view of gay relationships as "disgusting" and "dangerous"; and both views contribute to the oppression of gay people. Today these people can be hospitalized and "treated" (electroshocked!). They can lose their jobs, their legal rights, and their social position simply by being identified as gay. Psychiatry and the therapy fields have furthered the notion that homosexual behavior is a "character problem"; the courts have made such behavior a crime.

Therapists have developed all sorts of sophisticated conditioning and deconditioning devices for "treatment" (abolishing) of homosexual behavior, the goal being to restore (healthy) heterosexuality. Thus therapists have encouraged the oppression of gay people and encouraged them through intimidation to stay in the closet, to pretend to be "normal," or to change their sexual behavior. All this has further alienated and harassed gay people.

In our culture, gay people are the brunt of cruel jokes. The worst name anyone can be called is "queer." Women in the women's movement have remarked that the worst insult men choose to throw at them is "lesbian." Gay people are seen as comical; they are also feared as dangerous child molesters—this, in spite of the fact that the great majority of sex crimes are committed by straight males against young girls. The image of the homosexual is one of our culture's heaviest bogeymen. They are always supposed to be ready for sex, ravenous and cruel, debasing, lewd, dripping with depravity. Actually, this caricature is an excellent portrait of the straight world's own unconscious attitudes toward sex as a nasty and dirty commodity for sale. If gay people share in it at all, it is as Americans, not as gay people.

The gay liberation movement has challenged all this. It has demanded that gay relationships be legalized, that persecution and "treatment" of them be stopped, and that their sensuality be recognized as legitimate and fulfilling. Disruptions at therapy conventions by gay militants have had nationwide publicity.

Gay relationships have opened up sensuality. Gay women have written eloquently about sensuality as a non-orgasm-directed activity. Gay men have discussed the liberating sense of being able to love other men without having to compete with them. They have openly discussed men expressing feelings freely and warmly—hugging one another, crying, accepting their own gentle aspects instead of playing socially dictated macho roles. All this causes anxiety in the straight world.

Sometimes gay people demand that everybody explore and express cos gay side. Often too there are subtle and not so subtle power plays within gay relationships, the same dominance/submissive behavior that exists in oppressive straight relationships. This is not a sign that gay relationships are bad, or that everyone has to go along with whatever the militants demand. All relationships in this society have the capacity to be turned into power games; and many people, especially in the straight world, have long demanded that everybody else follow *their* brand of sexual orientation. The roots of this can be traced to individualism, the massive insecurity in this country, and the craving for power at others' expense, which marks most of the interpersonal relationships we all go through. Gay relationships can be as oppressive as any others when they fall into the same old traps; and gay people can be oppressive when they judge straight people as "sick" or as lacking in revolutionary ardor unless they go along with being seduced by a militant gay. But these two modes of behavior have existed for years and years in the straight world, and are in no way peculiar to gays.

We should be clear about the ways gay people are oppressed in this society and about the role that therapists play in this oppression. At the same time, we need to be critical about what the gay movement advocates and not support everything it says just because it is a "liberation" movement.

In this sense we have to point out that the gay liberation movement often seems to lack an understanding that sexuality, like all other phenomena in this society, is a manifestation of a class society.[8] We have to clarify what, in the gay movement, serves the interests of the working masses in this country and what serves the interests of alienated petty-bourgeois people. This is a difficult task, because feelings on this run very high.

We have to understand, for example, why it is that homosexuality flourishes in some epochs and societies but not in others. Historically, male homosexuality has reflected ruling-class notions that women are an inferior sex and that sexual relationships between men are a "higher" expression of love. Is this so today? How much does the gay women's movement make men the "enemy" and thus divide the working masses in this country at a time when the class struggle is sharpening. How much does

[8]These views are mine, not necessarily the co-author's.—MG

gay liberation represent an attitude of not struggling, men with women, over the issues which affect them both. How much, then, does homosexuality represent an individual attempt to deal with a sexist society; how much does it deflect people from directing the blow at the real enemy, the U.S. ruling-class.

We also have to be critical of the way the gay movement has helped divide the women's movement in this country. It has been one of the factors keeping working-class women from entering the women's movement, because sexuality rather than class oppression was put forth as most important.

Many things are "fun" which feel "personally liberating" and which "don't hurt anyone." But this is no test of its being in the service of the revolution. (Drunkenness or promiscuity can be these things, too.) We have to be able to speak out clearly against the persecution and victimization of gay people; and at the same time we have to speak out against the continued preoccupation with sexuality as primary, to the exclusion of the sharpening class struggle.

In dialectical terms, this means understanding what is bourgeois and what is proletarian in the gay movement: opposing the one and supporting the other. After all, in our dying imperialist country, signs of deterioration into individualism and sensationalism are everywhere. We have to be clear what moves us forward and what holds us back.

7

Marriage and the Family

We are experiencing a new interest in the family. For years therapists saw individual patients only. They acted as if their patients' friends and families were nonexistent, projections, or irrelevant. If couples or families were having difficulties, they were seen by ministers, medical doctors, social workers, or friends. Lately, though, top-dog therapists have moved into the area of family therapy with great enthusiasm. The past two decades have seen couple therapy, marital therapy, family therapy, and family group therapy emerge as respectable and lucrative fields. Spurred by research into the dynamics of families with psychotic children, family therapy now justifies itself by calling the *family* the "sick" unit, thereby freeing the individual from that burden. In practice, this is more accurate than focusing only on individuals. But the family therapists are now starting to peddle reactionary notions of family life, love and marriage, male/female sex roles, and the place of children in a family to a captive audience.

For therapists, seeing families is more interesting than one-to-one treatment. There's more action. In most therapists' hands though, family therapy is another way of influencing people in the same old way.

Therapists get little information during training about

family structure, about the social/political/economic basis of the family and about the kinds of jobs most working people have. With little real experience in interpersonal relationships—even less beyond their own class experience—they wind up accepting traditional bourgeois notions of marriage and family life. In liberal fashion, they see their role as "improving communication" among family members, alleviating family scapegoating, and establishing harmony. Their approach is symptomatic: They rarely question the nuclear family as an institution, the legitimacy of marriage, or the assumption that other kinds of intimate living groups are pathological.

In psychiatric residency, when we interviewed a patient who had lived in a commune, the staff automatically assumed that to be a mark of "psychopathology," a deep dependency problem, a strong antiauthority dilemma, and so on. Recently, we have found that when members of a commune seek counseling, the therapists almost always assume that the communal environment is sick, not supportive. Therapists share (and shape) American cultural stereotypes; they haven't had the proper experience to understand different ways of living. Their own lives and values are middle class, and they can't and won't free themselves from them. Thus they regurgitate society's generalizations about family life to their patients. Exceptions aside, their role is generally reactionary.

NUCLEAR FAMILIES

We Americans have lived in tight "nuclear" families—parents and their immediate offspring—for a fairly brief time, one or two generations. Yet this is widely taken as the best, and probably the *only* way of raising children. Beneath this ridiculously crinkled scab lies an unhealed sore many layers thick.

In earlier years, the family was much larger ("extended"). It might easily include three or four generations living together as well as some family friends. Ties among people were close, but tensions were diffused. Others were available to be intermediaries in disputes, to form alliances so that people weren't isolated or scapegoated. Family members fulfilled one another's needs; no one or two people had to shoulder the burden of the whole group unless there was severe difficulty. Henry V. Dicks has quoted the Russian writer Gladkov to describe the traditional family:

A peasant homestead, ruled over by his old grandparents, with father and mother and uncles and aunts, siblings and cousins living together under one roof, seated at the table in hierarchical order, working and praying together, the women strictly subordinated even to the youngest male—all obeying grandfather in awe and piety. There was nowhere to escape to, no industrial town in which to seek alternative work for the rebel sons. There was no freedom to move except to court the girls in the village over the hill. The brides were selected for the lads by arrangement between parents—a dowry passed. The new daughter-in-law was now under orders from her mother-in-law. They all tilled the fields and celebrated the harvest. Opposition was put down harshly by the old man, and his adult sons, who were also his laborers, begged for forgiveness on their bended knees. For Grandfather's authority, like that of the Father-Tsar's, was from God.[1]

The traditional family followed strictly authoritarian lines, under religious sanction. This fit the economic needs of that time—many people clustered under one roof. Illness, poverty, the need for cooperation, the sense

[1] Henry V. Dicks, *Marital Tensions* (New York: Basic Books, 1967), p. 15.

of hierarchy, united state, town, and family into a consonant whole. No other choices seemed available. The world was narrow but secure. If people sensed their oppression, they had few sensible alternatives, and their awareness did not lead them anywhere.

Postagrarian, postfeudal families entered the cities and maintained the many-generation structure for a time. Then, the grandparents' authority began giving way; younger men (but not women) found they had more options. People moved out and supported themselves, no longer relying on the family except in times of crisis. The family became more and more mobile. Great industries, employing thousands and thousands of people, provided housing for them and shipped them from one plant to another taking over grandpa's role. The family became stripped down to a set of parents with their fairly young children. As soon as kids could leave the home—go to college or to work, join the army or get married—they split. The aging parents saw their lives dwindle down to just the two of them; ahead lay a solitary apartment (apart-ment), trafficking from child to child for visits, or the nursing home.

The typical family now consists of two parents and their kids; perhaps too a growing number of postdivorce families, with single parents and kids. Grandparents are elsewhere, and so are aunts and uncles and grown-up siblings. Some cultural groups—Puerto Ricans, Italian-Americans, blacks—have different kinds of families, more in line with the traditional extended family. This seems to hold for people in third world groups, but not for white America.

Nuclear families are very important to our economy as units of production and consumption. People living apart means more dishwashers, TVs, cars, record players, refrigerators, stoves, toys, bathroom fixtures, furniture, kitchen implements, children's clothes, and so on. It guarantees that more and more money will be spent on "necessary" items which, if people lived more cooperatively, would not have to be so endlessly duplicated.

112

Nuclear families lay tremendous psychological demands on their members. Mother and father must fulfill a whole panoply of emotional needs: Husbands must be good providers, pleasant and effective fathers, handymen, good lovers, disciplinarians, jolly faces able to undo their wives' tensions, and—beyond this—productive members of society. Wives must be housemaids, child rearers, doormats and pillows for their husbands' tormented heads, good in bed, organizers of daily recreation and activity, excellent shoppers, socially active, and always in a good, productive humor. One of the harshest burdens falls on the kids. Not only are they supposed to grow up and do their share of fulfilling the family's expectations, but also they must grow up helpless, dependent on their parents, seeing themselves through their parents' eyes. This makes them closer and more vulnerable to their parents. The emotional pressures become intense, especially in middle-class families, where the mothers and fathers "live" for their children. So much is poured out in the name of love for them that the kids feel tremendous pressure to perform. After all, when so much has been sacrificed/given to them, they must show their appreciation by repeating or bettering the family pattern, respecting their parents and elders, living the good life their parents could be proud of. The family oppresses every member; few are freed from its economic or psychological domination; few escape the rage, guilt, impotence, and profoundly ambivalent feelings that the family generates or get beyond the need to recapitulate somehow their family-of-origin, even though they know how damaging and destructive such a family has been to them. Thus, kids wind up like their parents, and nuclear families keep going.

What is the family for, anyway? What do we judge its success by? Human beings need to be cared for when they're little, and people need relationships with others that meet their emotional demands. Marriage and the family are ways of satisfying these needs. Legal and institutionalized, they bring society's approval with them. All other ascribed functions of marriage/family are probably nonsense, after the fact rationalizations. They can be fulfilled elsewhere, in other ways.

Loving and caring *do* arise in families: We hope we're not misunderstood about that. Of all the alternatives we have now, the family more consistently generates warmth and affection, more often cares for its people when they need help. The family also creates much brutal treatment, torment, hate, and despair: much of this is due to its function in society, not to people's being together. Our society has made the nuclear family an instrument of exquisite torture.

Why do we live in families? Because we ourselves were raised in them, because we feel odd trying any other life style, because we rarely think about alternative ways of living with and raising children. Once we strike at our tradition we are striking at our male culture, at capitalism, and at American imperialism. We start a revolution.

Child rearing is a profound area to explore. Few others, besides mothers and occasionally fathers, step forward to care for kids. Not even in the most freewheeling communes do radical-chic people volunteer to take over the burdens of infant and child care. Yet most nuclear families manage to give children a basically supportive atmosphere. We have seen communes where the single people avoid any part of child care, except to demand that the kids stay quiet and out of everyone's hair. We have seen communes which simply would not accept people with kids. We have seen women who were active in the women's movement refuse to help other women with kids because they felt it was none of *their* business, in spite of the "sisterhood is powerful" myth. We have seen divorced men totally abandon their children to their ex-wives, even though they continue to write and talk the most "revolutionary" politics in town. Until other forms of child care show stability and promise, most kids will continue to be raised by nuclear families and by loving (possessive) parents.

We have seen communes split up after a few months; we have seen people move in and out of them. To kids, such comings and goings are confusing and extremely upsetting. Kids need some stability; they need at least one continuously present adult in their lives for emotional support. Without this, kids grow up troubled and suspicious, frightened and impulsive.

We all need others. The family, for all its oppressiveness, offers fulfillment of many of our needs. It offers emotional support—often reluctant and uneven—but support nonetheless. People are near who care about us, who spend time and energy with us. Until we can develop ways for intimate relationships to attain some kind of stability, some kind of trust, we can expect people to find it through the more legal/stable pattern of marriage and the family.

Some of us are now experimenting with intimate relationships outside the legalistic framework of marriage. There is a greater chance for freedom in an equal relationship, a better hope for liberation. But the search also involves profound anxiety, mistrust, jealousy, fear of separation, and a sense of the impermanence of most human relationships, which adds to the already heavy burden of trying to create changes in our social institutions.

With this said, though, the problems of marriage and family remain as great as ever. Fulfilling certain needs, they nonetheless brutalize us, imprison us, and deaden our sensibilities. Often we blot out such awareness of our disappointment, for fear that we can find nothing better.

Our fantasies about what love/marriage/family should provide are limitless. They are the driving source behind our current songs, pop fiction, films, conventional magazines, TV and radio programs, and our day-to-day conversation. These fantasies and expectations are far beyond the reality of what people living together in tight, small units can provide. They do not jibe well with the constant pressures of debts, schools, social obligations, work, isolation, and boredom. It is no wonder, then, that most of us feel cheated, disgruntled, disappointed—no wonder that divorce rates are moving toward 40 and 50 percent. Marriage and the family simply can't provide what they promise.

People in the United States now move about rapidly, living under pressure and incessant demand, masks and shadows, uncertainty and risk, impermanence and isolation, and mistrust. They cling to what they can find—a marriage, a child, a home, a job. The outside world is a wicked, frightening, dangerous place. We have created a paranoid world (and should not be surprised at encountering a number of paranoids in it). But the cost of clinging to the family for security is seen in wasted lives, exhausted and destroyed women, competitive and frightened men, confused children; damaged, spent, and despairing people.

MARRIAGE

A lot has been written about marriage, but it boils down to a few simple statements. People usually marry for common reasons: The woman is pregant, the couple wants to find security or get away from their parents, the couple is "in love" and marriage is the next logical step. Marriage is seen as a cure-all for people's problems—a way of finding security, sex, intimacy, and a life purpose. The problem is that it often doesn't turn out that way.

There's no denying that we need relationships with others. Life is lonely and alienating, we feel chronically unsure of ourselves and crave closeness with others. The mass media, our parents, and all the books we ever read have conditioned us to expect a solution in marriage. The

116

catch is that marriage is a cut from the same social pie as the rest.

When we finally realize that marriage has just placed us in another demanding, confusing social situation, we get angry and resentful, depressed and hopeless. Sometimes we then end the marriage, blaming the partner for having made it so messy; sometimes we just grit our teeth and stick with it, deciding that it's bad anyway, and we should get used to it and work out what we can. About one-third of all marriages now end in divorce, and this figure is rising; other marriages wind up trying to save themselves with wife and husband swapping, open-marriage techniques, sex manuals, group sex, and so on. Then, when all else fails, the "now" parents say they are staying together for the children.

Much of this comes from the gap between the ideal and the real. Marriage for love, which used to be the fantasy of the privileged few, has now become the institutionalized goal of every American teenager.[2] Parents and the media encourage this. Sex education and problems-in-living courses continue in the high schools, but most young people still act as if sex attraction and being in love must automatically lead to marriage. Parental attitudes, encouraging guys to marry women they've "gotten into trouble," don't help people postpone a decision to get married and so add to the problem. Some of this may be changing with the pill, the option of abortion, and the knowledge that people may fall in love several times in several years. Unfortunately, the awareness that the tasks

[2]A discussion of romantic love and its long history is beyond us in this book. The reader can find it in Denis de Rougement, *Love in the Western World* (New York: Pantheon, 1956); Shulamith Firestone, *The Dialectic of Sex* (New York: Morrow, 1970); William J. Lederer and Don D. Jackson, *Mirages of Marriage* (New York: Norton, 1968); Simon de Beauvoir, *The Second Sex* (New York: Knopf, 1953); and Betty Friedan, *The Feminine Mystique* (New York: Norton, 1963).

of marriage are different from the demands of a romance becomes part of young married people's experience.

The wish is an old one: People want to find the Magic Mate, the Missing Half. Idealizing one another, they stop being honest and open about themselves, thinking that the Marvelous Other will reject their weaknesses. Feeling inadequate deep down, each of us imagines the Other is *really* adequate. Thus the game of mutual deception and illusion unfolds itself, with each partner hoping to continue fooling the other. Everyone stays insecure, everyone is always uptight, and at some future time everything bursts out in a shower of blame and fury.

Couples often marry, each partner expecting the Other to be the Ideal, perceiving the Other as in fact the Ideal, and each trying cos best to *act* like the Ideal the Other wants, figuring that the only way to land the Ideal is to act like the Ideal's Ideal, even though each knows co isn't really the Ideal.

For example, Betty, who grew up in a family with an overbearing father and weak, browbeaten mother, has determined to be a free and independent woman in her marriage. She chooses Will, a man who appears genuinely soft and gentle, understanding, artistic, permissive. In the relationship, she acts strong and confident, taking her share of responsibility, helping to make decisions, feeling like a genuine partner. Will, who grew up in a family similar to Betty's, has resolved not to be the kind of bully his father (and older brother) was; he also has promised himself not to settle down with a weak, vacillating woman like his mother. So he finds Betty attractive because she can stand on her own, let him relax and not always have to be the boss. Each seems to satisfy the other's wants. They court, love each other, and get married.

A little later, they begin to have arguments. He has begun to get upset when she denies him sexual access, feeling it is his right, after all, to make love when he wants to. In addition, she has begun to get on his nerves because she wants to keep on working, even though he feels fully capable of making enough for the two of them, and would *like* her to stay home and keep the place clean and start friendships with other women in the neighborhood. He also expects her to cook him dinner, which she resents strongly, remembering how her mother wore herself out day after day preparing meals, cleaning house, running after the children.

Then, after a disagreement, Will's brother calls, and asks Will what the hell is wrong with him, why doesn't he lay down the goddamn law to Betty. And Betty, in a tearful conversation with her mother, gets told that, after all, what did she expect, marriage is marriage, and Will isn't such a bad guy after all, so she will just have to learn to swallow some of her stubbornness (always a bad character trait in a woman), and become more considerate.

Betty realizes that Will's softness and understanding is a cover for his feeling insecure, and that when he is threatened, he becomes hard and demanding, placing his own self-interest before hers. For his part, Will feels that Betty's "strength" is really a castrating and harsh trait, and he wishes she were more "feminine." He feels less sexually attracted to her, but more compelled to "prove himself" sexually upon her reluctant body. So they argue more and more.

He starts to act like his and her father. She tries to deal with it, but gets no support. Finally, one night, she throws a hysterical screaming fit, just like her mother used to, feels guilty and ridiculous afterwards, but doesn't know what else to do.

The scenario can end in various ways. They can split. They can decide to have children to "bring them together," as her mother suggests. They can go to a marriage counselor who will tell Betty to learn more wily seductive techniques and encourage Will to "give her a little more say in things," perhaps a few evenings out together, and a hobby or club for Betty to get interested in. Or they can decide to stay with each other, but hating each other more and more—drinking perhaps, or having some affairs, or getting hooked on television and family gossip. It happens every day in millions of homes.

In such a context, people often go to a therapist to try to "work things out." What can *therapy* mean here? Usually, it means focusing on the interpersonal situation, on the inevitable distortions each partner is pushing on the other, on the feelings of hurt and inadequacy, on the needs each partner has; on the secrets, on the faulty ways of communicating needs and feelings, on the necessity to work harder as "partners" in the relationship, on the different families each partner has come from, and on how different cultural/familiar perspectives have added to the quagmire. Yet with all this emphasis on the relationship, "therapy" almost always ignores the overriding realities the partners live with: the unequal power distribution, the culture-bound expectations for marriage, the different role choices available to the couple, the politics of their class position. Solutions are offered that are tailor-made to the couple's own situation. But they are solutions that ignore the institutions of marriage/job/family as agents of oppression, and instead encourage the couple to adjust sensibly to the reality around them.

This is how therapy acts to cool people out, isolate them further, encourage their individualistic thinking and their overemphasis on personal fantasies and personal histories—in short, to keep them functioning in society. A politically oriented therapist would relate the personal/emotional problems to the partners' position in society, to the jobs or nonjobs, to the oppression they experienced growing up in families, to the discrimination and pressures they face in day-to-day life now, to the racism and sexism of contemporary culture, and to the effects of U.S. imperialism. Rather than emphasize their personal feelings, such therapy education would interlink feelings with political realities. To our knowledge, only a few heroin treatment programs offer this degree of political education in their treatment. All other therapy is antipolitical (reactionary).

Another example is Art, who drives a bus for the Metropolitan Transit Authority, and is having "marital difficulties" with his wife Brenda. They've been together for four years. She has a daughter from a previous marriage; he'd never been married before. Her daughter is with her ex-husband, she's upset about it. Their problem revolves around her wanting to spend time out by herself —his feeling angry at this and retaliating by going out by himself with the "boys." They own their home and are trying to buy a better one in a more fashionable suburb. Art's parents, to whom he is very close, still disapprove of Brenda and discourage her visiting them on the Sundays when Art goes there. She feels resentful and claims that he loves them more than her.

It is easy enough to focus on the personal differences. Art is the youngest of six children, and has always been close to his parents. Brenda is the oldest of three, and has always taken care of herself. In her family, people are outspoken and spontaneous; in his, they are calmer, more self-contained, and repressed. When she is flamboyant, he becomes threatened; when he is moody, she takes it as profound sulkiness. Much of their behavior and feelings comes from their different family styles.

But other realities are there too. Art's job exposes him to the values of other working-class men, who tease him for being pushed around by his wife, who encourage him to go out with the guys, who play cards for relaxation, go bowling, hit the bars. Money is hard to come by, and Art actually has a good job, with the chance to pick up extra cash by working overtime if he needs to. Efforts of a family therapist to change Art's way of relating to Brenda, to help him to loosen up and be less demanding, less petulant, and so on, expose Art to further ridicule among his co-workers and from his family. Brenda, on the other hand, uses the therapist's encouragement of her assertiveness to push Art even further, thus pulling him away from friends and family.

Here middle-class therapy values clash with working-class experience and place a great strain on the already fragile bond between the two. Art's feelings of impotence and inadequacy become worse as the therapist proceeds to talk circles around him and charm Brenda. Gradually, he withdraws from therapy and accuses Brenda of being unfaithful. Soon the two stop coming to the therapist, but they have solved little and have only exposed themselves to someone they found they couldn't trust.

Brenda has not been given the chance to work some of her feelings out with a women's group; instead, she has been encouraged to play sexy games with the therapist. Art has been placed between two cultures and asked to relinquish some of the little sense of power he has, exposing himself to ridicule from everyone he knows. The realities of their jobs, their community, their families, their home and financial problems, their expectations— have all been ignored.

Marital relationships are often sparring matches, open or covert. The partners argue over power and control, self-esteem, and sexual privilege. Children, when they enter the picture, easily become foci of scapegoating and guilt.

Because of their extreme dependency on each other, the partners often can't attack each other without jeopardizing their main source of support. Only an eventual alliance with another—a lover, a close friend, a relative, a therapist—permits them to be brusque and furious. They resent not being able to express their feelings and having to fake things; they handle their resentment by making life miserable for each other and driving each other crazy. One day, unable to tolerate the charade any longer, they explode, or collapse, or go berserk. On that day everything falls apart. But instead of bringing a healing reaction, this often only brings further collapse and destruction.

If they can hold together through this process, understanding that, yes, they depend on each other but cannot control each other through guilt and coercion, there is a chance they can pull back a bit, allow a healthy distance to come in between them, become more self-confident and self-controlling. In such a process, they become more whole people and they are also better able to live together.

If they cannot hold together and split, there's always a chance they'll go on to repeat the same pattern, but this is a chance they have to take. There's no a priori virtue in holding on to the marriage or the family past the point of hopefulness, past the point of too much pain.

Children get drawn into this morass, as pawns of the parents. Growing up is a difficult task, especially since kids in our society are told to pretend what they don't feel, to forget what they know, to forget the act of forgetting, to pretend they are not pretending, to believe they have not pretended or forgotten. They are told to act correctly and to repress and cover over their real feelings. There is thus the split between real (inner) self and behavior (outside-acting) self, the core of our society's schizoid personality. Put this together with the need to placate authority, and the character structure prevalent in a fascist, authoritarian state becomes clear.

We have all forgotten the real brutality of those years. Healthy children can get some relief from it by joining peer groups, by entering fantasy, by blotting out the oppressive present. For this they need free space somewhere—either in their family, or in the outside world; if not there, they will find it inside their heads or they will rebel.

The compulsively monogamous marital twosome and its offspring, cut off from other people, isolated from any relevant political/social action, becomes a rancid swamp —a grave. It swallows people and drowns them.

Most people stay married and stay with their families. They deal with the conditions of their lives by drinking, taking drugs, buying whatever they can afford, having affairs, burying themselves in their work. Many of them preserve a sense of self by working diligently, caring in some way for their children. At least they are not "failures." At least they are good citizens, loyal, religious, responsible. And the oppression they all labor under continues, fueled by their sacrifice, their blood, their tears, their suffering. They drive themselves to exhaustion preserving the shell of a relationship whose innards have rotted.

It's no wonder the parents are threatened by the freedom of young people. If the young can actually change the misery everyone lives under, this will undercut all their parents' sacrifice, acquiescence, passivity, and failures to move on what they believed. Sexual freedom, new thoughts, optimism in the face of social opposition: all these make the older, mature, and resigned generation quiver with indignation at the youngsters' gall.

That explains in a way why teenage kids are suddenly presented with overwhelming parental control: new rules, new prying, new interdictions, new injunctions, new dictates to dress modestly and behave correctly and cut their hair and take no drugs and be in before midnight and hope they don't get pregnant and of course never take birth control pills, and so forth. They are free to do anything except challenge the authorities and make trouble.

The older generation, acting in the interests of the ruling class, makes war on the young. It tries to bludgeon and kill them, eat them, and re-create them in its own image: clean, correct, God-fearing, upright. It tries to make them atone for its own myriad of sins.

The nuclear family, devouring its members' life force,

creaks on like an old subway train in a tired and dirty city: swaying, rambling, lurching, stopping and starting, polluting—but not fixed.

A NOTE ON CLASS AND FAMILY

The literature of therapy focuses on the problems of white middle-class people. So too its techniques: verbal and intellectual insight-oriented therapy, groovy body-movement work, encounter shake-'em-up stuff, and so on. It's important to realize that therapists have almost totally ignored problems of minority groups and working-class people, lumped them together as difficult-to-treat people, and given them drugs for their woes, state hospitalization for their inability to cope, and referrals to other agencies for their unruliness. Various studies have shown how therapists prefer to work with people of their own social class, and how they see much more "pathology" in people from lower social classes than from their own.

Family therapy usually discusses the middle-class, achievement-oriented family, with bright clever kids and confused but articulate parents. These families' incomes allow them to go into therapy; their values let them see it as potentially helpful. Thus the recommendations for "open communication," "learning to argue better," and "learning to share the chores together" are aimed specifically at the middle-class family.

Let us simply point out here that different kinds of families exist in this country. Welfare families, for instance, and families of unemployed people or migrant workers, are pitted against the world (and often against one another) in a struggle for survival. These families often are more extended, multigenerational, with less emphasis placed on simply husband/wife/children. Often the family is not "intact": Husbands are missing, dead, or never home. In some black families, a grandmother may be present, the father gone. Families that have to scrounge for work, day to day, have little energy for issues of affection, romantic love, and "open communication." There is a struggle for food, for living space, for private space (often one of the biggest complaints of a young person in these families is the lack of personal space and the constant feeling of being intruded upon), for some source of self-esteem. On the bottom of the social pile, this group is directly threatened by drug use, prostitution, violence, assaults, and robberies. Their lives are uncertain and often beyond their control. They have few real options; thus, they feel powerless and passive. Their role in society is to form small productive and consumption units and a reserve labor pool.

Working-class families are a bulwark of support to the working masses in their struggle for survival. Their tasks are often overwhelming. The oppressiveness of many working-class families is due to their having to provide all the nurturing functions for its members, in the face of the constant attacks from the ruling class. Working different shifts, scraping about for money, always on the verge of economic difficulty, these families spend their days trying to sustain their members.

Sexism, placed on the backs of the workers by the ruling class, has a bad influence in many families. Sex and job roles are often rigid, and the men are threatened by the thought of abandoning traditional male roles. Much of this is a result of their position in the economic structure.

These families are forced to struggle for survival day after day. They function primarily as economic units—production, consumption, mutual support. Because of fewer options, their lives are continually insecure. Therapy, to them, is a middle-class thing, alien and threatening. By and large, they are correct to be suspicious of therapists and to stay away from the mental health centers except in times of dire emergency.

Middle-class and professional families also reflect

126

the social norms—upward-striving, accomplishment-oriented goals, sexual liberation to some degree, affluence and consumerism. As a class, these people "believe" in therapy and are its staunchest supporters. They want their children to be well adjusted so they can succeed; they want to be "in touch with their feelings" so they can be happy; they want to be able to take advantage of the privileges they have. Politically, this class is liberal when someone else's interests are at stake, and reactionary when their own interests are at stake. Much of their family problems revolve around their children, who form the predominant element in today's youth culture and counterculture. Youth-culture values conflict sharply with middle-class values: leisure versus work ethics, open-ended versus closed-off ethics, drugs/music/pleasure versus performance ethic. The impact of youth culture and some of its alternatives—food co-ops, communal living, drugs, natural foods, emphasis on the here and now and spontaneity—has the potential to undermine seriously the traditional middle-class posture. This will be one of the foremost areas of struggle over the next years —and one in which therapists, working with families, can be agents of change.

LOVE, ROMANCE, AND INTIMACY

Most people go from one day to the next, one struggle to the next, one paycheck to the next. Their concern is to survive, to have a few kicks, to blot out the pain. A few try to "create" something, but they usually give up soon enough. Even so, most preserve a sense of romantic love. Most people have experienced it at least once in their lives, and regard it, especially when it is mutual, as a highest good, a beautiful feeling in itself. And so it really is.

Falling in love can be called an "escape," a hideaway,

a way to avoid the world's dilemmas, a way to remain with fantasy. And yet it can also be a surreal, transcendent experience, rich and ennobling, liberating, overwhelming, freeing us for thoughts and for an openness with others that was not there before. To be close to another, open and resonant, we wouldn't knock that experience. We wouldn't "analyze" it, just as we wouldn't "analyze" away a poem, a dream, a painting, a religious experience. The experience of being in love is one of those sublime experiences, mystical and awesome, which words cannot satisfy.

Let us quickly add that in this society romantic love has become a stereotype. Once it was the privilege of wealthy ladies mooning for their lovers. Today romantic love is everyone's fantasy, the incredible cure-all which is supposed to reintegrate us as people when we feel alienated and incomplete. In this society, we are so quick to convince ourselves that we are in love that we barely have time to sense what we sense, feel what we feel, know what we know. The romantic myths don't reflect today's reality.

So, although there remains a potential in us all for romantic love, we overvalue it, search for it all the time, and leap at it before it's there; in general, we are careful not to do anything else. Work toward sensible goals is left behind, living in intimate ways (not always sexual) with others is abandoned: No time for that. The one-to-one, so productive when the lovers are involved with the world, as well as with each other, falls apart. All that's left is a clinging towsome, or, worse, wishy-washy individuals staggering about looking for the Magic Mate.

Since, as Shulamith Firestone points out,[3] only love between equals has a chance of succeeding in this world, a really satisfying romantic love relationship requires a lot

[3]Shulamith Firestone, *The Dialectic of Sex* (New York: Morrow, 1970).

of work. The couple needs to work hard at abolishing the usual sex roles, the usual power trips, the usual dependencies. The partners need a focus in the world as well as their feelings for each other. Otherwise, even a sweet and loving romance will turn to sand, helped to its demise by oppression, manipulation, mutual fears, and the destructive intervention of others.

There are other kinds of love. The love of parents for children and of children for parents, the love of close friends for one another, the love and admiration of student for teacher and teacher for student. Religious feeling and love of humankind are also love experiences we're not talking about here. It would be foolish to denigrate these feelings, to reduce them, to imply that they are incomplete or inauthentic. The range of human sentiment is large; any aspect of it may be deep and fulfilling. No single relationship can be expected to encompass it all.

A lot of foolish material has been written about the different kinds of love. Yes, we can experience sensual/sexual love that absorbs us totally and opens up other levels of experience to us; we can call that Eros. Yes, we can experience a caring, spiritual affection which does not necessarily have to include sexual components; we can call that Agape. Yes, we can experience feelings for others we know in limited ways—people we work and struggle with, comrades, people in our houses. We have no real name for those feelings except "love." Love is not exclusive in this sense. A one-to-one relationship involving sexual feelings may preclude other sexual relationships—or it may not—but it certainly does not forbid other very close relationships and feelings. The stranglehold that many current monogamous relationships put on its partners is deadening and destructive.

We become fools if, idolizing the romantic love relationship, we forget the other relationships that surround us (or that could surround us if we would allow it). Many of us, when we have no romantic relationship in our lives, spend our lives worrying about one. Many of us, when we are involved romantically, spend our lives absorbed in it and only in it. It's rare to find us integrating such a relationship into living, caring, and working with others. A romantic one-to-one can be a cornerstone of relationships in the world; but it becomes sour if it is isolated. A very good way of avoiding the sourness today, if possible, is for people to live communally. We can thus depend on others, relate with others. This is crucial if we are to escape the deadening "only" dependency of the one-to-one in isolation.

Shulamith Firestone's sixth chapter in *The Dialectic of Sex* opens up the contemporary discussion of love's psychopolitics. She shows how men use falling in love to maintain their security via holding on to a woman. The emotional flow, she feels, is one-sided. She wonders if men are even capable of loving—they seem so rooted to exploitation and oppressiveness, always preening their sagging self-esteem. Women get little from the love relationship, except—hopefully—security. For a man, loving is tied into possessing; for a woman, with establishing an identity in a man's world through relations with a man.

The feelings of being attracted to another, of being in love, are good and nonoppressive in themselves. It's what we do with them that mucks us up. The power difference underlies our dance: The man, choosing his woman, tries to obliterate the power difference by elevating her to the level of the Romantic Object. The woman, sensing what's being done, reacts cautiously, moves slowly, not risking her own security. Firestone feels woman's frequent "clinging" behavior is socially necessary—women can't risk spontaneity or frankness without (usually) jeopardizing their man's approval.

Of course, men themselves are victims of this game. Though they are not usually as crushed as women who play it and lose, men stand to lose their self-esteem, their self-image, their overblown and puffy view of themselves. They conceal themselves from the world, competing mentally and actually; they hold themselves back and risk only what they know they can afford to lose. They know how to withdraw quickly, to turn the tables on the woman. They can easily play the conquerer, the sure one, the strong one. Women, by contrast, are cast in the role of "lucky to be loved," a position (pedestal) they can easily fall from since it's not under their control to be there. They're there only as an act of magic/grace. Although men can lose favor in their lovers' eyes, they are not (realistically) so devastated as women whose lovers/mates leave. (As I write this, I'm not at all sure this is so. It seems so. Women in this society tend to be simply more vulnerable than men, even men who have taken the risk of opening up. When men are hurt, they still have survival skills, they are still "men." Women who hitch their star to a man are wholly lost if the man leaves. That's the importance, it seems, of a woman's gaining financial independence, other friends, mobility. It's no accident that women have wedding rings and trousseaux; they need these material possessions as security when their loving man decides to take off.)

All this materialistic/survival orientation is important. Still, there's another dimension of relating to another. The surrealists had a notion of *l'amour réciproque,* which differs from the usual teenage American romantic ideal. Such a love, as André Breton explains it,[4] is between equals, and is a way of experiencing our deepest selves, of exploring ourselves and our lover, of reaching out for our dream images, our unconscious images, our temporal and spatial patterns which we'd forgotten were locked within us. The experience is like countless doors, which we thought were locked forever, opening up, each with a different treasure behind it. The experience unlocks our

[4]André Breton, *Les vases communicants* (Paris, 1955).

potential for living. Such a relationship fuses the real and the fantastical, and shows that the two were not opposites in the first place.

Susan Beth, writing about Breton, summarizes his attitude toward love:

The strongest and most complete love is, for him, the love that demands unity, not with some abstract divine perfection, but with another human being. This love must function on both the physical and spiritual levels of existence. . . . For Breton there is more beauty to be found in [love's] "infinite possibility" than in any final crystallization. In this possibility . . . are the sources of man's revolt against the limitations of his condition, and of his ability to communicate with his universe and his fellow man. . . .

At all times love must realize itself through a participation in the real world.[5]

We have to understand why such relationships seem so difficult in our society. Is it the nature of the relationship, or something in our competitive, fast-moving, self-centered world that sabotages and cramps the free, spontaneous interchange?

Time and again, the power difference corrupts and destroys relationships. Perhaps people who get together out of pragmatic mutual need rather than out of "love" have an edge: They make no pretense at what they want; they are not setting themselves up for disappointment—only for struggle. But even these pragmatists fall into the oppression of power difference. They form their own rut, whether it's over who should discipline the kids, or who should carry out the garbage, or who should write the checks. Anger and mistrust grow; genuine moves for closeness become abhorrent to the psychopolitical frame-

[5]Susan Beth, "The Theme of Love in the Works of André Breton" (Ph.D. diss., Columbia University, 1967).

work and are rejected or used against the person taking the initiative. Each partner negates, dehumanizes, manipulates the other. Mutual blame, mutual guilt, mutual laceration result.

Just as Firestone wonders if men are really capable of loving, so we can wonder how many long-standing two-somes are capable of genuine affection and responsibility. Of course, many such couples appear fine, deny any problems. Who are we to say?

We know that our society produces emotional cripples by its rigid prescription of behavior; we know how compulsive monogamy (marriage) and the family can destroy people; we know how material circumstances can make two people irritable and exhausted, in spite of their loving each other; we know how sexism can poison relationships by turning them into battlefields. But we also know of the potential for love and togetherness that exists in us all. This is the aspect we want to encourage. As people begin to attack the old repressive forms, we can all build on our strengths—mutual concerns, common politics, collective struggles—and develop new, satisfying relationships among people.

CHILDREN

Children in America grow up in nuclear families: helpless, small people, barraged constantly by the damaged products of cultural oppression—their loving parents. Our authoritarian, hierarchical society creates people who define themselves in relation to power: They obey orders from those above them while demanding obedience from those below. The inherent sado-masochism in this situation destroys both (all) parties. Resentments aimed at those with power over us cannot be expressed except as oppression handed down the line.

Wilhelm Reich delineated the effects of this social order on its people, especially the children. His analysis remains true today:

The foremost breeding place of the ideological atmosphere of conservatism is the compulsive family. . . .

The child cannot escape a sexual and authoritarian fixation to the parents. It is oppressed by parental authority on the basis of its physical smallness alone, whether this authority is strict or not. Soon, the authoritarian fixation drowns out the sexual one and forces it into an unconscious existence. . . .

The basis of the middle class family is the relationship of patriarchal father to wife and children. He is, as it were, the exponent and representative of the authority of the state in the family. Because of the contradiction between his position in the production process (subordinate) and his family function (boss) he is a top-sergeant type; he kowtows to those above, absorbs the prevailing attitudes (hence his tendency to imitation) and dominates those below; he transmits the governmental and social concepts and enforces them.[6]

Children are more victimized today, for their mothers have also become representatives of the state's morality, consumers with an interest in the status quo, angry, depressed, oppressed individuals with deep ambivalent attitudes toward the children who make them mothers.

Children have little choice in most families. It's up to them to adapt, to preserve their sense of self however they can, if they can. Their lives are regulated by external social institutions—schools, TV, parents' values, songs, advertising, papers. They are fed fairy tales and myths about what women and men, girls and boys are really like. At an early age, with pink and blue ribbons and blankets, their differentiation and socialization starts.

[6]Wilhelm Reich, *The Sexual Revolution* (New York: Farrar, Straus & Giroux, 1970), pp. 71, 76, 73.

134

They swallow what they are fed: Later, some may spit it out, from down deep in themselves, but at risk of losing their stomachs in the process.

Parents, impotent and confused, follow the media, the teachers, the experts' advice on how to raise their kids. Middle-class, individualist norms are forced on everyone, even kids from other classes. Kids who don't go along with it are labeled "problem children" and (with their parents) are given instruction in the hopes of changing their behavior. Kids who persist in defiance will wind up tranquilized, in reform school, in foster homes.

The aim of this is to prepare another generation of nine-to-five people whose values include punctuality, hard-working performance, docility toward superiors, dependence on *things* for status and happiness, a sense of people as things and possessions, an acceptance of sex-role myths, color-linked myths, gay-straight myths, American-foreigner myths. At a certain point, they begin to have some insight into what's happening; they begin to have a choice in the matter—and rebellion becomes possible. At this point, they may change their pattern, start acting differently, precipitate family crises—or go mad.

Many older people today are upset about young people. They refer to the "problems" of delinquency, drug use, and violence as serious "difficulties" in young people. We feel such "problems" need to be redefined. A teenager who has been offended, brutalized, lied to, and pushed around by schools all cos life may, on seeing this, be furious. Such anger, expressed in acts against the school, in destroying its property is reasonable—it may be the first sign of a growing awareness. Kids who band together and act against the social order, which has obliterated their identities for years, are not guilty of "inappropriate behavior": They are ready for further political education which will offer them options other than entering their parents' world.

Drugs can cripple kids if used to the point of addiction;

but drug use is also, phenomenologically, an expression of anger at the world of the kids' parents. Since the ruling class has the power to define what is right and what is wrong, it takes care to define behavior that threatens it as "bad." One task for revolutionaries is to *redefine* people's behavior, underlining the aspects of struggle and challenge in day-to-day situations. For many people, an antisocial act may be their first break with oppressive and dehumanizing cultural values.

Kids, for instance, begin questioning what they've been taught—not talk with their mouths full, cover their face when they sneeze, keep clean, smell clean, brush their teeth, clean their plate, make their bed, straighten their room, share with others, give in to others' commands, keep their knees together, don't talk back, keep their lines straight, shut up—and try to get in touch with what they really feel deep down, where all the feelings have been demoted, suppressed, laid to rest, covered over. Their questioning cannot, though, be too threatening to their parents and other authorities. Perhaps the parents can dismiss them with comments about their age —"too young," or "that's the age when people start talking about those things." The result of most of this is that the kid realizes which side cos bread is buttered on. That is, the kid senses co can be left and abandoned, and just might be, unless co plays along with parental values and behavior. Often, we find, the "psychotic" patient speaks the truth to the family and finally cuts through the games and mutual deception, pseudointimacy, cant, and so forth. But at a very high price.

Kids are born omnipotential. Their lives are gradually channeled for them, more and more narrowly, until finally they seem like a recognizable character type— neurotic, or a crazy off-the-wall person. It's the tragedy of this society that kids must lose, day after day, year after year, contact with their feelings, their dreams, their fantasies, their potential for having fun, being serious, being alone, or being with others. After all, except for a few peers, who is on their side? The media, the schools, the older generation, the cops, business, the government, the army: everyone tells them to grow up, stop whatever it is they're doing, and take on their parents' (the transmitted ruling class) values.

The issue of children's rights is just emerging. In this society, children—people below eighteen—have almost no civil rights: They are forced to go to school, regarded as their parents' property, and can be sent to mental hospitals or special schools at their parents' or other authorities' discretion.

One young man, picked up by the police in Massachusetts for possession of marijuana, was given the choice of facing charges or getting "professional help." His parents committed him to one of the state's private mental hospitals that specializes in electroshock treatment, inflicting it on over 95 percent of their patients. The young man got about a dozen treatments before he was finally released. Other stories like this, usually including electroshock as a matter of course, or as a punishment for resisting the "tranquilizers" prescribed by the treating psychiatrists or for "making trouble," are commonplace, if anyone takes the trouble to listen.

This is, of course, one reason why some political groups have chosen to work among disenchanted working-class or alienated middle-class youth. Such work directly attacks the notion of children as parents' property and undercuts transmitting ruling-class culture through churches, schools, boys clubs, Girl Scouts, and so forth.

Children are their parents' offspring; they will not change unless others affect them—classmates, teachers, new friends. One revolutionary task is to help bring young people new experiences and new ideas. We need to help them fight what oppresses them; we need to help them develop meaningful options.

Aspects of education, free schools, community schools,

sexual liberation, and sexual information are beyond the scope of this book. But they are important in reaching people who may be of age when this society undergoes its revolution.

Therapy's role in working with couples and families is often to reinforce the traditional oppressive patterns. We are too cynical at this point to believe that "enlightened" therapists are now going to lead their clients to social/personal change. Perhaps the answers lie in the whole task of "detherapizing" therapy.

8

Alternatives and Alternate Life Styles

Many people feel the oppressiveness of the way things are, and agree about the need for change. The kinds of changes they propose, though, differ widely. One recent development, affecting primarily young people and disenchanted white dropouts, has been the move toward a "counterculture." Salvation and meaning are found in the pursuit of an alternative life style, which encompasses anything from natural foods to being honest about your feelings, from rural communes to rock music. Terms like counterculture have become so broad that perhaps we should define them before going further.

"Alternative life style" usually refers to people's wanting to change the entire way they live. Thus there is an emphasis on (1) living collectively instead of in nuclear families, whether in urban or rural areas; (2) sharing skills so that people are less dependent on the "straight" economy—for example, starting food co-ops, learning auto mechanics and first aid, forming work collectives; and (3) dropping out as far as possible from the "straight" social and political units, with the goal of becoming self-sufficient. Thus alternative life-style advocates are often utopian in their orientation, putting forward the theory that, if enough people drop out and pursue alternatives, the capitalist system will collapse of its own inefficiency and tediousness, and society will be transformed. Because most of these people come from affluent, middle-class families they can "afford" to drop out. Because they tend to scorn straight aspects of life like jobs or nuclear families they often alienate working-class people. Some of these people, though, are trying to involve themselves in the struggles of working-class people. The term thus covers both actively political and antipolitical (reactionary, romantic) people.

"Counterculture" is also used to refer to the efforts of people pursuing alternatives. The "culture" involved, though, includes such things as rock music, interest in pure/natural foods, use of drugs, interest in Eastern religions and mysticism—yoga, Zen, Tarot, *The I Ching*—and an often deep value placed on taking things as they come, keeping cool, and maintaining an inner peace. At times, counterculture is used to refer to the hippie/groovy scene, at times, only to young people. This—like the others here—is a media term, used mainly by radio, TV, and "culture commentators"; they are grossly generalizing and specify very little.

"Youth culture" is used to refer to where young people are: drugs, rock music, fancy clothes (hip capitalism), and so on. There are some very political groups in youth culture—Rising Up Angry in Chicago, for example—as well as many young people unaffiliated with any group, whose tastes and goals in life have been shaped by the culture merchants of the youth culture. Here it is important to understand that young people, like everything/everyone else in this country are a *commodity*, used and manipulated for profit. Youth culture cuts through traditional class lines.

It's become fashionable today to take part in the counterculture by smoking dope, being "honest," and trying to get a place in the country. The rationale of Consciousness III points up the way in which many people would really like to see social change occurring—spontaneously, without social struggle or personal risk. The counterculture myths support this idea and thus co-opt—taking out of the struggle by buying them off—people who might otherwise pursue less heady goals. We want to be careful not to lump the utopians and suburbanites and fashionable people together with those earnestly pursuing alternatives with a political perspective. The latter group has a sense of the risks involved, the long-term nature of the struggle, and the need to organize broad elements of this society for such a task. In other words, there are revolutionary as well as counterrevolutionary elements in the "counterculture."

The primary task is to transform society. Such a task can be approached on many levels, fought on many fronts. At this point in time, it appears that organizing on several levels, working in revolutionary collectives, and perhaps even establishing a new political party is important. New alternatives will emerge, some of them responsive to political needs, some against them. Right now, people are pouring a tremendous amount of energy into the search for viable alternatives. A lot of energy is needed. It's important to evaluate each project, and to understand which aspects in it further social change and which are obstructive and reactionary.

We know that, where possible, it is important to change and convert existing institutions so that they serve people's needs and are under their control. This can involve factories, hospitals, school systems, department stores, supermarket chains, day-care programs, and so forth. Where such change is not possible, we will have to destroy old institutions and replace them. Such a struggle means that a large part of the alternative culture is in inevitable conflict with the ruling class in this country—opposing its rules and values, its institutions, its morals, and the part of its values which we have all incorporated within ourselves as our own inner-oppressor.

Of course, we do not support *all* "alternatives" simply

because they are different. The Jesus Freaks and the KKK are "alternatives" too. We need to define which alternatives are part of the problem and which are part of the solution. We cannot sanction a cultural laissez-faire that encourages everyone to "do their thing." We support alternatives that enhance people's political consciousness and lead them ultimately to face the necessity for revolution in this country.

LIFE-STYLE ALTERNATIVES: DROPPING OUT

Much of the drop-out scene is limited by the age of its people. People drop out for a time, and then get tired of it. People go off to the country while they are young, unmarried, without kids, then leave to become "straight." Of course, some older people are now dropping out too, starting communes and collectives; but the majority continue to be the young.

A lot of the life-style movement reflects class privilege. White middle-class people, becoming hip and aware, drop out of their parents' institutions. They get into dope, natural foods, together relationships—and then often jump back in again. They often remain very isolated from the communities of working people who live around them. Groups that make a go of it, incorporating political awareness into their lives, relating to people around them, seem to fare much better.

But alternatives often fail. We need to be open about that too. Collectives fall apart from in-fighting and taking on more than they can handle. People have money problems; they get angry and jealous, isolated and exhausted after days of constant struggling. Possessiveness and competitiveness continue to be our social/personal heritage, making genuine efforts at change difficult and constantly a challenge.

When an "alternative" falls apart, it demoralizes the people who were in it, and encourages the defenders of the status quo. "See," they say, "you just can't fight human nature." Or, "those people were so far out, they couldn't do anything together." Once we understand which alternatives we should support, we must find ways of really helping them stay alive—in terms of personal support, techniques for being open and honest, and whatever other aids to their struggle we can provide.

YOUTH CULTURE

For a while it seemed that young people were going to join the political liberation movements. Street politics and rock festivals seemed to be coming together. White working-class youth became the focus of overt political action (by Weathermen), with hopes of bringing new strength to the political struggle. Some of this succeeded. But the early hopes now seem to have been overly optimistic. Today we see young people sliding back into class privilege when they can or joining the rat race to improve their position. They are aware of the contradictions in this society, and they do not like what they see, but they feel powerless to change it.

Rock culture, always sexist, has shown a recent potential for encouraging fascist behavior too. Violence at rock festivals, especially against women, is combined with macho swagger and fights. The drug scene is more and more into heavy mind-numbing drugs—downs, smack—which totally sap people's potential for struggle, and which remove them from any political scene.

For example, at the American Legion Meeting in 1971 in Portland, Oregon, the planned political protest was undermined by the city's sponsoring a free rock concert, miles from the Legion parade, at the same time as the planned demonstration. The kids, full of dope and love for music, wound up by the thousands at the free concert; only a few hundred people showed up for the political demonstration against the Legion. The establishment's power to co-opt and contain youth culture seems to be matched by the young people's lack of political awareness. "Doing your thing," the transience of the scene, the "hip capitalists" who make hundreds of thousands of dollars from rock concerts, records, fancy clothes, dope dealing, makeup, incense and funny posters, groovy lights, glossy magazines—all sabotage the attempt to organize street people. Money gets ripped off the young as the price of "being groovy." And the money goes right to the people who control America, to support the same old shit, the same old public sell and image making.

Many free clinics and rap centers which sprang up to "serve" the street people of the youth culture—acid freaks, potheads, up-and-down addicts, juice freaks, smack freaks—have spent an incredible amount of time in social welfare band aid-type work. Time and energy get poured out on a population no one else wants to treat (unless they get a government grant for it), and the kids take off for the next town as soon as they can get a gig together. By providing such an "alternative" service, freak centers relieve the obligation of the established institutions—hospitals, clinics—to deal with socially caused problems. To make matters worse, the alternative institutions often become as bureaucratic and hierarchical as their "straight" counterparts. Because they don't often have as many trained people on their staffs, they at times succumb to even worse authoritarian pressures. Who does this serve?

The developments in 1972 at Sanctuary in Cambridge point out how an alternative street clinic became institutionalized and tightly controlled by a few people (men), and then pursued a tight medical model of people's emotional problems, quite, "psychoanalytical," due to the unchallenged and unchallengeable position of its only M.D.

psychiatric consultant. Other such innovations, begun in a collective spirit, saw their togetherness fall under the burden of grossly unequal salaries, power hierarchies, infighting, and professionalism. The kids are served poorly, if at all, and another institution is born.

The same thing is true of Project Place in Boston, where a struggle now seems likely between revolutionary and bourgeois notions of "alternative" service. Supported by liberal foundation and federal funds, Place is vulnerable. If it becomes too "radical," it loses money; if it pulls back, it winds up reneging on all its ideals. One visible consequence has been the growth there of utopian (back to the land, let's do it in small groups) encounter-group attitudes and their work is the essentially white life-style problems which avoid political confrontation.[1]

In addition, the "street culture" is changing. Instead of the flower children of the mid-1960s experimenting with marijuana and LSD, the kids are now involved with heavier drugs. The sweetness and light is gone from the scene: Predators and con-men have infiltrated the street and exploited its people to their own ends. Instead of affluent but disenchanted middle-class kids, the streets now contain alienated working-class kids too. And alcohol, which used to be shunned by everyone, has been making a big comeback. The Free Clinics and rap centers, which can now boast of being institutionalized and accepted and funded by the U.S. government, are attempting to serve a population which no longer exists. Their liberal motto of "everyone do their thing" and "we're only here to help" leads to a supertolerant professional stance; so long as the helpers' professional status is unquestioned, they will go along with almost anything. When, in the end, the street kids turn on them with a fury, they appear totally perplexed.

One of the most global attacks on the counterculture

[1] See Michael Glenn, "Crisis in Counter-Institutions," *Radical Therapist* 2, 6 (1972).

came from Lynn O'Connor. Writing in *The Woman's Page*, she attacked it from a class-conscious woman's perspective. Her main thesis is that the alternative culture, with its emphasis on new life style and innovation, is the same old "monster in disguise," especially regarding women. She sees it offering another form of enslavement, instead of fantastic liberation.

The counterculture, she points out, relies on class privilege. For its women ("groovy chicks") life becomes even more insidiously oppressive: they are told to go back to the kitchen and take care of the cooking and the kids, to be exciting sex partners—perhaps for more than one man, the ultimate in "liberation"—and great earth mothers. Yet they don't even receive the minimal material advantages straight society offers: wedding rings, legal protection, good medical care. The counterculture, for all its emphasis on change, is extremely macho. We have gone into free clinic after free clinic with women and found them targets of strong anti-women's liberation talk and jokes. The exploitation of teenage women by the drug and sex merchants has been very destructive. The men who say "our chicks are really liberated, man," usually mean that "their" women are their property and don't challenge that status.

O'Connor also points out that the fads of natural food and hip clothes tie the counterculture into more and more expensive, and thus middle-class, consumer patterns:

The latest Horatio Alger fantasy to The American Scene is something called "alternative life styles" or the "counterculture." All across the country the young men and women are living in communes instead of nuclear families, trying to make a living off of handicrafts instead of taking corporate jobs, throwing bricks through government windows instead of joining the Young Democrats, or getting stoned instead of getting drunk, consuming at the Goodwill instead of at Sears, eating brown rice and vegetables instead of meat and potatoes, ripping off the supermarket instead of stealing from the family business. They think they can avoid the agony and boredom and meaninglessness of their parents' lives by these so-called "different" ways of doing things.

The stated purpose of the alternative life stylers is to escape from the horrors of the larger society by ignoring it, dropping out, and building one's own little world with a counterculture, counter social and economic institutions, and of course counter people. Ideologically identical to the system they wish to escape, they believe that an individual or small group of individuals can in fact "make it" just because they want to. They believe that it's possible to live in the middle of a cesspool and remain uncontaminated.[2]

This bares the crux of the argument against the counterculture: that its attempts to create "alternatives" are irrelevant and based on class privilege and a poor sense of what kinds of political changes are needed to transform the society. Essentially utopian, they abandon the masses of people who don't quite have their class privilege and go off to "do their thing."

Such a critique does ignore some groups in the counterculture who concern themselves with larger social change. Urban communes, which draw people together to work politically, give one another emotional support, and collectivize consumer patterns, definitely challenge the usual pattern of urban isolation. Rural groups of people trying to learn and practice farming skills, to establish food co-ops, to pursue crafts and handiwork, involve themselves in the day-to-day workings of their small-town communities, in the squabbles over school systems,

[2] Lynn O'Connor, "Counter Culture: The Monster in Disguise," Supplement to *Radical Therapist* (June 1971).

and in efforts to make life less expensive for their neighbors by sharing. Then too some counterculture people
have earnestly tried to change their sexist patterns,
whether in groups or in their intimate relationships.

The dangers of the counterculture lie in its liberalism.
In accepting everything, in encouraging individualism, in
not analyzing people's options politically, the counterculture winds up moving everywhere at once, and nowhere
at all. It becomes a social not a political movement. Such
a wishy-washy supertolerant attitude has obvious results:
Goals are never reached, small groups collapse for lack of
clear direction and commitment, and people play power
games with one another.

The alternative life-style movement does have revolutionary *potential*—the same sense of nature, space, and
freedom of the back-to-the country people: the concern
with environment—inner and outer—that the pure-food
people express; the new awareness that mind-expanding
drugs have brought; the feelings of community that communes and collectives have demonstrated. We must understand why these elements have not been cooled out
instead of fired up; why political consciousness has been
squashed instead of stimulated. To us, the answer lies in
the class nature of the "alternatives" movement.

DRUGS

Although the street people have now turned to harder
drugs, one effect of the counterculture has been to raise
people's awareness of their own potential. Many people
have been changed by smoking grass: The sudden time
shift, the mind-tripping, the sensory euphoria and relaxation and goalless enjoyment have been profound experiences for uptight people whose lives until then had been
dominated by performance and achievement goals. The

psychedelics have pushed this process even further: They have shown people through direct experience how limited their day-to-day lives are, and how vast an area of mental and sensory experience lies open to us, could we but free ourselves from the tyranny of our "Civilization." People with such drug experience are less likely to accept a set of values that emphasizes ego control, acquiring objects and social status, and "adjusting" to the limits of life. Though we certainly do not support people's mashing their brains into mush through chronic or intemperate use of drugs, or copping out of struggles by nodding out, we do understand how a drug experience, when it is integrated into one's life, can be a powerful incentive to further change. It is no accident, we feel, that the government has made war on marijuana and psychedelics, while actually encouraging the use of heroin and turning completely aside from the mass use of barbiturates, quaaludes, and other soporifics. The government tolerates drugs that dull people and keep them from struggle, but drugs that open up people's eyes are called evil and dangerous poisons.

MYSTICISM

Part of the counterculture fad involves a taste for mystical and irrational experience: Tarot cards, *The I Ching*, yoga and meditation, trances, hypnosis, Eastern religion, ESP, alpha brain waves, magic and witchcraft, demonism, astrology, palm readings, cosmic "energy" and interpersonal "vibrations," primitive light/darkness religions, and other occult phenomena. Much of this is garbled with escapism and wishful thinking: the irrationalism which comes from sloppy thought and a quest for easy solutions. Some of it reflects a healthy attack on conventional rationalism, and the belief that "everything can be explained rationally." An interest in the occult, when it brings forth mysteries of human experience which our repressive civilization tries to keep in the dark, has a progressive aspect: It confronts us with the sterility and barrenness of our intellectual framework, and bares the contradictions in human experience, which we ordinarily try to forget—the vast power of the nonverbal to move us, the mysterious dialectic between Yin and Yang, between light and darkness, between aspects of ourselves, the power of our dream images and of our collective visions. When it is used as simply another "far out" thing to dabble with, the mystical is misused.

The great "mystics" of the past—Saint Teresa, Saint Catharine, Saint John of the Cross—used their mysticism to keep in touch with the world of real (political) experience, not to withdraw into their own heads. If we want to imitate their appreciation of the otherworldly, we ought to imitate too their immersion in the struggle for social and political changes.

GROOVY THERAPIES

The new wave in therapy today is the "humanist" movement, which incorporates the "self-growth" centers, new body techniques—Rolfing, bioenergetics, massage, touch-feely—sensitivity and encounter groups, marathons, Gestalt, primal therapy, and so on. The group, obviously, is quite diverse. Yet for all their differences the group members share an approach—against the psychoanalytic tradition and for a new mind/body integration and permissiveness, and for the affirmation of "self-actualization"—that is, the importance of people realizing their true potential. Of course, such aims endear them to the middle class and the young who can afford the cost of their weekends and groups, and who find individual solutions difficult to come by in an age of alienation. The movement has mushroomed in the past decade. There's fantastic booty to be made in selling/facilitating "self-realization" to the affluent and disenchanted, the young, the businessmen, the industry captains, police leaders, school personnel, and so on. Played straight—that is, facilitating "communication" among dissident groups in industry, government, schools, and communities—such work can bring in money or prestige. Played countercul-ture—operating wild, permissive, "honest" groups among the young and alienated—such work leads to ego-tripping rewards: personal power, manipulation of others, sexual benefits. That the status quo has so quickly lapped up the human potential movement—the use of Bethel and Esalen as consultants to the industries which oppress this country, the use of encounter groups to cool out tensions on the job among racial groups—should make us wary of what this movement is all about.

The Association for Humanistic Psychology, parent organization of many of the self-growth groups, held its annual meeting in September 1971, in Washington, D.C. Its theme was supposed to be the dialogue between social action and personal growth; the meeting copped out. Its slogan suddenly appeared: "Power to the Person!"—an incredibly arrogant parody of the revolutionary slogan "Power to the People!" The panels were individualistic, self-indulgent, and irrelevant. "Social Issues" included panels on whether therapists should sleep with their patients, how women could "become" people, and alpha brain waves of "alienated college students." The thrust of the meeting was toward even more far out head-trip and body-trip experience, with a minimum of attention paid to "social" involvement. It's no accident that most of the founders of the AHP have since left the organization, which seems lately to have become a haven for every kind of groovy quack and touchy-feely roué in America. It's not as funny as it sounds: the AHP commands tremendous resources and "professional" prestige.

The humanists and Gestaltists promise self-knowledge,

"finding yourself" in a society where no one knows coself. By their challenging the old traditions of psychiatry/psychology, they have helped focus on the sexual/social repression which traditional therapy serves to maintain; by opening up body experience and emphasizing concern with other levels of consciousness, they have helped move beyond the confines of talking or drug therapy; and they have shown important enthusiasm for the potential of groups. For this, we support them. But we cannot support their being co-opted, bought and used by our ruling class to neutralize potential change by focusing people on solely personal and intrapersonal issues, and ignoring social/political realities. This is the danger of the touchy-feely movement.

Thus we are opposed to the use of therapy to continue oppression, mind fucking, and egotistical power tripping; but we encourage the new movement to explore the limits of people's feelings and sense experience. The sensitivity movement, Gestalt, encounter, bioenergetics, Rolfing: all these have a profound potential for integrating our heads and bodies. Used self-indulgently, they are instruments of a decadent society; used to bring people together for collective work, to support them in challenging the status quo, they can be revolutionary tools.

It infuriates us to see such valuable and powerful tools used for individualistic purposes: experience-hungry freaks of all ages dabbling in one profound pool after another, muddying the waters, learning nothing they will share with others. If this sounds like a put down, it is. We are sick of the AHP types making a lucrative living at the expense of the people. We are sick of hearing people "rap" about heady mystical ideas for hours on end with no concern for the jobless people next door. Some people have gone overboard on self-centered nonsense, and, in the end, their sweet ego tripping has meant other people's getting fucked over—Vietnamese dying while the Esalen freaks get to Level 6 or talk about the "positive growth experience" of being crazy; black people being shot in the ghettos or third world children dying of lead poisoning while the children of the white middle class talk about their latest Tarot reading. This must be called what it is: turning one's back on the world and supporting the system's bloody policies through indifference.

LIBERATION

There's a difference between "freedom," the license to do what you want as an individual, and "liberation," which implies a sense of political and psychological control over one's own life, shared with others' being free from oppression. Freedom alone—the word itself may not be the best or only word, but this concept is crucial —means the ability to have some privilege for oneself— being free to move about in society, being free to try this or that. Liberation involves us all in the struggle to end oppression, political/social/psychological, and in any other form in which it exists.

In this sense, we need to be aware of pursuing alternatives that fight oppression and ultimately liberate us. And we need to beware of supporting programs that only increase the privilege of a few people to indulge themselves in new experiences. Just as we have seen that "sexual liberation" or "alternative life style" can become a farce if its "liberation" is derived from continuing or furthering the oppression of others.

RAP CENTERS

Rap centers are one therapy alternative (usually for young people) which has spread across the country. Originally, they began as part of the Free Clinic movement in

San Francisco and Berkeley, and spread from there across the country as alienated young people brought their cultural institutions with them. They offered a place to "get it all together" without being hassled, a place to get good free advice and counseling, and a place to keep out of the cold and rap with friends. Many centers began as the creations of the street people themselves; later, groups of professional, "concerned" people, often with community support from the elders of the town—teachers, policemen, judges, physicians, ministers—established "rap centers" with groovy outasight names as places where the kids, especially those with drug problems, should go. The "kids" the centers were for were usually middle-class white kids who had been getting into trouble smoking dope or sniffing glue or getting pregnant.

Clinics started by black and brown people have usually stuck to community medical/political/health issues, and have not gone extensively into counseling. Working-class people still appear to distrust counseling and therapy; and, as most of the rap centers offer professional (liberal) therapists who are doing their therapy thing in a now-swinging setting (which means very little is different from seeing them in their plush offices), they are probably right to be mistrustful.

Lately, some of the community leaders, following the line set by the nation's leaders, have been focusing their youth programs on drugs and violence. Drug use has now been designated not only a crime but also an illness. Mental health professionals, entering the political arena, co-operate by labeling kids who smoke dope as "sick" and can, with legal/court/parental help, stick the kids into treatment programs or even into state hospitals. Kids who become delinquent are seen as dangerous and sick; their delinquency is not analyzed as a symptom of their awareness of their oppression, or as an attempt to grapple with it. Nor are their schools/families/churches/clubs looked at to see how they have become oppressive and alienating institutions. Instead, the kids are labeled "sick" and carted off to treatment programs.

Many rap centers today, rather than being programs set up by young people to meet their own needs—feeling lonely, needing a place to rap, a place to stay—are programs set up by adults to treat and contain rebellious kids whose sexual/social/aggressive/drug behavior totally threatens and embarrasses the adult world. The use of Synanon-type techniques to further assault adolescents is another new additon.

In North Dakota, for example, drug use is seen as an illness. Kids who are found guilty of a drug offense are encouraged to go to one of the Awareness Houses recently brought into the state by their promoters in Arizona. Awareness Houses use Synanon-type group/assaultive techniques on kids to help them recognize their own deep, personal problems that have, by making them "sick," led them to drug use. At such places, they are "treated" by a group of groovy professionals in accordance with the board of trustees' wishes—the board being community adults with a sprinkling of kids. They are told they are "sick" and "dependent," their drug use is but a symptom of personal problems. They are encouraged to challenge one another, to grow up and become independent—in short, to accept their parents' values and return to their schools, families, and communities and be like the others. Their home milieus are rarely questioned. For kids who challenge this soapy approach, the state hospitals are available; and release is virtually impossible for a sixteen-year-old kid whose angry parents, school officer, minister, and judge have agreed to commit co to the hospital's adolescent unit. Mental patients' rights are already inadequately maintained; the rights of young patients don't exist at all, and their efforts to find a lawyer or another psychiatrist are also impossible. Most of them, in our experience, wind up pretending to be "cured" just so they can get out. They learn to be manipulative and psychopathic—good defenses in a manipulative and hypocritical/schizoid society. The pattern in this state is being repeated everywhere.

Rap centers that kids control usually get into serious trouble. The community becomes quickly threatened. The coffee shop or meeting place or rap center is closed down amid rumors that drugs are being peddled, or that orgies are going on upstairs, or that the people there are all anarchists. The wall posters are pronounced "offensive" and un-American. The kids' language is called crude. Whatever the rationalizations, the community, threatened by kids controlling their own programs, dries up the program's funds and shuts it down.

Many rap centers that serve kids, then, have trouble simply staying alive. They can get money and ample community support by telling kids that drugs are bad, that they should straighten up and walk right. But such cooptation usually makes the kids abandon the place. The few rap centers—like Sanctuary in Cambridge and Project Place in Boston—which do stay alive, often wind up having interminable hassles over their own structure. As they grow, they develop their own professional cadres: social workers and psychologists who have committed themselves to alternate institutions and who now are reluctant to share their knowledge or give up their power and control. Splits often develop between the kids themselves and the staff which is "serving" them, and even between the volunteer (nonprofessional) staff and the paid staff. Problems of institutional growth/hierarchy/identity become all-pervasive, and the group's vitality is often compromised. Government grants and subsidies from private foundations often have corrupting strings attached; and when, without such money, the rap center has to fold, the group is faced with choosing between selling out or collapsing.

The business of a free clinic or rap center should be to put itself out of business, to help transform society so that people won't need the center. Instead, rap centers—like all other institutions—wind up with staffs and jobs and the desire to grow and perpetuate themselves. Such a task is made difficult by the rapid turnover in staff too. The commitment to rap centers as an alternative appears transitory for most young people, professionals, and nonprofessionals.

OTHER ALTERNATIVE INSTITUTIONS

Food co-ops are an alternative way of buying fruit and vegetables (sometimes meat and fish) by utilizing the collective buying power of many people as contrasted to the relative helplessness of the single supermarket customer. People spend incredible amounts of money on food today, but groups who shop together, buying directly from the food producer, can save up to 50 percent on their food bills. It is a way of providing nutritious, fresh food at cheaper prices, and of helping organize a neighborhood, especially a welfare or working-class neighborhood. As such, a food co-op is valuable. Often, though, the only people in the co-op are radical or alternative life-style people. The other community people, though they may be invited, are not encouraged to join; nor is their own experience respected by the others. One food co-op in Charlestown, Massachusetts, had a good number of welfare families, almost all of whom left after a superrhetorical group of "radicals" paraded around with Viet Cong flags and anti-American statements without really explaining their politics to the people. This kind of fiasco has been repeated in many places.

Parents want better and cheaper food for themselves and their children; everyone resents being ripped off by supermarkets. If food co-ops can move to include people besides radicals and freaks, they will be able to raise community awareness about nutrition, the politics of food consumption, and so on. This way of working for change, especially in urban areas, needs to be encouraged and explored further.

Day-care co-ops have been the focus of much effort lately. Once again, though, working-class people have been somehow discouraged from participating. Still believing that mothers should stay in the home, they are wary of middle-class efforts to pull them out of it. Others, who are working already, have made less rhetorical arrangements with friends, neighbors, and relatives to care for their children. They are mistrustful of the sudden appearance of middle-class white women heralding "their" cause; they are mistrustful of women's liberation because they see it challenging their economic/emotional security. The men, who are often oppressed by their jobs, do not respond readily to wifely demands that they do a little more housework or take the kids one or two days a week.

The as yet unanswered task of the counterculture is how to cross class lines and make its alternative available and attractive to working-class people, as *they* wish to use them.

Free universities and free schools are other such efforts. Education under consumer (student) control, or education under the control of the parents' community instead of the administrators, is vitally important in a community that is trying to pull itself into the struggle. The same difficulty of including working-class and welfare people in such programs instead of affluent middle-class people, exists here as in other alternative programs.

Jobs are a challenge to the counterculture. Many of its people still have to work in the "straight" world and "live" on their free time. The counterculture is poor; it's constantly being ripped off by drug pushers, hip capitalists and so on. It does not offer many jobs—except individual handicrafts and the like—to its people. And few of the jobs it offers pay a living wage. One of the problems of building new institutions is supporting them and the people who run them. Thus many people go on welfare, try to live on $2,000 a year, and rely on (liberal) charity for subsistence. Their political power is thus diminished. Dropping out seems associated with subsequent political impotence and apathy.

Groups like Vocations for Social Change, various professional groups, and community organizers are trying to develop alternatives for people that can support them. To date, it's not clear how well they will succeed. Certainly, the material poverty of the counterculture is one factor in encouraging people to leave it as they get old and have families.

Underlying the search for a new life style is the conviction that the way you live your life is a political issue of prime importance. Talking radical politics is meaningless if you live like a pig and treat people like shit. If you oppress the people you live and work with, all your talk about "liberation" is shallow. But concentrating on a life style that reflects your politics is hard work and involves giving up a lot of privileges and habits.

COMMUNES

Communes are one alternative that has really caught on. In the Boston area alone, there must be 150 to 200 communes of varying types. They offer people a chance to live together, thus attacking the isolation and individualism of American life. They offer an opportunity to have friendships beyond the one-to-one monogamous situation, to move out from under the nuclear family, and to find others who can provide emotional support. In addition, the expenses of living communally are less than living alone.

A group of people living together can become an extended family. If the reasons for being together go beyond a boardinghouse mentality, there's a genuine chance for a loving, growth-supporting community to develop, thus making it possible for people to carry out difficult and exhausting work without being totally devastated by it. People can eat together, work together, share tasks, help one another, and grow closer.

There are a multitude of different communes, some from a sexual freedom viewpoint, some from a get-into-yourself viewpoint, some like a boardinghouse, some from a political/collective unity. It's hard, in many parts of the country, for any kind of commune to exist. Landlords won't rent to communes; welfare denies surplus food to people living with young, unrelated people; and neighbors manage to harass young communes and spread the most incredible rumors about them all over the community. Few communes are affluent enough to buy their own house. Communes that include political activists can expect police harassment and even drug busts and raids. Zoning laws, welfare laws, and the natural curiosity/resentment of others make it hard going.

Not all the difficulty comes from without. Many communes have been wracked and destroyed by inner tensions: arguments and power squabbles about money, control, and sex. Some of the trouble comes from our naïve hopes that we can quickly find a viable alternative that will work wonders without much effort. We have all been raised in nuclear families, have all grown up in a sexist and racist country whose exhortations to us are to succeed, to push ahead over anyone who gets in our way. When we finally decide to try to change these patterns, we must expect it to be tough going.

Living together with other people like ourselves is hard. Interpersonal problems are worsened with more people, not lessened (although the intensity of some one-to-one relationships may be lessened in a communal context). Many members devote hours each day to the smooth running of the commune, to handling interpersonal problems, and settling disputes. Such time can be a real drain on people's energy and patience, especially if the same disputes keep cropping up—sexual jealousy, money rivalry, differences over matters of taste, problems making collective decisions.

Often too, in the absence of a clear personal and political orientation, the recruitment and selection of commune members can be a haphazard business, leading to lengthy worries about incompatibility, about rip-off artists who are irresponsible and unresponsive to the wishes and feelings of others, about learning to share for the common (and individual) good.

There is also the problem of people pushing themselves too far too fast in trying to change old patterns without understanding the depth of their emotional tie/dependence on them. Thus people have tried to smash monogamous one-to-one relationships because of some ideas in their heads, and then find it's a horribly upsetting experience emotionally, perhaps something they don't even want for themselves. The use of movement rhetoric to generalize about "human" experience and cover over all individual differences has led many people into personal suffering and pain. For example, some people enjoy a multitude of relationships, perhaps with men and women both; others are strongly tied to a one-to-one relationship at certain points; and some who are casual and permissive can, at any time, become suddenly monogamous and possessive. All the rhetoric in the world doesn't change this fact. Rhetorical pressures to do what's right, all the time, make people feel guilty, confused, and inadequate —not exactly the milieu from which togetherness and social change will occur.

People in communes have become involved with sexual relationships and jealousy, and with the rhetoric of "collectivizing" everything, usually on some utopian notion that we are all interchangeable and equal. Recourse to collective rhetoric helps very little, and winds up pigging sisters and brothers for their feelings and situations.

Much of this can be traced to petty bourgeois origins. Acting on ideas instead of from experience, some members one-sidedly esteem personal relationships and one-sidedly ignore actual work and material conditions. They exaggerate the "cultural revolution" and try to make themselves models of new liberation. Their detachment from the realities of life hinders their development, and they often wind up picking themselves off the floor, having leaped too rapidly into situations they wanted to handle but couldn't. It's important for revolutionaries to have a sense of the *process* of change, to be patient and confident, and to support their friends' efforts to change themselves without trashing them.

If communes can at times be good, warm families, it's important to point out that they can also become as destructive as bad families—people laying trips on one another, exploiting one another sexually, manipulating others to their own advantage, pigging other people for their weaknesses instead of understanding them and helping them change; the commune itself doesn't prevent this from happening, but rather simply provides an opportunity for it to change.

Communes also have to meet the problem of generation. With all the rhetoric of how groovy it is to become an extended family, the fact is that most communes are composed of white, middle-class, young people who are unmarried and without kids. Bringing older people into the commune, or facing collectively the problem of child rearing are two "options" that many communes avoid, usually with the same self-interest rationalizations that you find everywhere else.

With all the awkwardness of communes, it's important to encourage the growth of such living arrangements, and to help those that have begun to deal straightforwardly with their problems. Every alternative that collapses from internal tensions represents a failure that might have been prevented, had its members understood a bit more about their own expectations, their own power trips, their needs, and their "process" of being together and growing.

People trying to make alternatives work will be facing extreme tension; they will feel isolated and persecuted, unloved, unappreciated. At times they will be withdrawn, paranoid, depressed. We need to understand this, to expect such feelings and not be thrown off stride by them. We need to help people be therapists to one another in times of stress and struggle, to support one another through such times without laying heavy rhetorical trips on them. Changing ourselves and society are not simply tasks, and pursuing them will take a lot of energy and emotion out of us. The hope of communes and other collective alternatives is that we can profit from one another's strengths and override our individual weaknesses through working together.

This can lead to fulfilling the common goal of those alternatives we support—creating viable political units which can challenge and change the existing order. Whatever can further this goal and create space in which it can operate autonomously should be encouraged and helped. The task will take many people operating on many levels on many fronts simultaneously. But it will succeed.

9

How to Be a Radical Therapist

An understanding of dialectics and the world situation helps us see that the fundamental contradiction in the United States today is between the few bosses and the masses of working people. Every institution, every person in the United States is affected by this contradiction. There are two lines, two aspects to everything. As Mao Tse-tung said:

The class struggle between the proletariat and the bourgeoisie, the class struggle between the different political forces, and the class struggle in the ideological field between the proletariat and the bourgeoisie will continue to be long and tortuous and at times will even become very acute. The proletariat seeks to transform the world according to its own world outlook, and so does the bourgeoisie. In this respect, the question of which will win out, socialism or capitalism, is not really settled.[1]

Therapy is a bourgeois institution in a capitalist-imperialist society. Its primary aspects, as we have shown, are bourgeois. It promotes ruling-class ideology. Objectively and subjectively it serves the interests of the people run-

[1]Mao Tse-tung, *On the Correct Handling of Contradictions among the People* (New York: China Books, 1966).

ning the country. The main task for revolutionaries who are now therapists is to resolve the contradiction between being a therapist and being a revolutionary. Historically, the weakness of the petty bourgeoisie lies in its vacillation from one side to the other, depending on its shifting class interest. Not rooted in the forces of production, not merged with the working class, therapists—as other petty bourgeois professionals—have a bourgeois aspect (freedom of working hours, some autonomy, no direct experience of oppression, good pay, a sense of creativity in work, individualism) as well as a revolutionary aspect. In fact, the bourgeois is usually stronger. We see the main task of revolutionary therapists as preserving their skills but changing their life situations. Just as Chinese intellectuals have been encouraged to go to the masses of workers and peasants, integrate with them and share their lives, so therapists who would work for revolution here are encouraged to do the same. Not to do so, to hold on instead to special privilege, is to widen the split between themselves and the masses, and ultimately to fool themselves into being "radicals" while the actual work of the revolution goes on elsewhere.

William Hinton has suggested that,

When they graduate, large numbers of students should seek work in basic production and strive, as communist intellectuals, to bring Marxism-Leninism-Mao Tse-tung Thought to the working class. In order to do this, they must live the life that working people live, join in the struggles that working people are actually engaged in, and then help raise these struggles, step by step, to the level of a revolutionary challenge to ruling class power.[2]

We agree with this priority. And it is only in this context of understanding—that is, to remain a therapist in this

[2]William Hinton, *Turning Point in China* (New York: Monthly Review, 1972), p. 110.

society is already to take the secondary, not the primary, road—that we go ahead with comments about how to advance the revolutionary aspect of what is mainly a bourgeois situation.

There are three aspects to being a radical therapist. One deals with ways in which people can be therapists for one another: self-help groups, knowledge and skill sharing, the acceleration of radical nonprofessional counselors, and so on. The second concerns ways in which people who are acknowledged "therapists" for their livelihood can act as revolutionaries and try to strengthen their revolutionary aspects while living with the contradictions of their life situations. The third aspect is institutional challenge and change.

HOW PEOPLE CAN BE THERAPISTS TO ONE ANOTHER

Most of the time, a professional therapist is not needed and does more harm than good. Therefore, it is important to develop ways and settings in which people can help one another, ways nonprofessionals can learn skills of listening to people in emotional trouble, clarifying the contradictions they face, and helping them deal with their situations. We feel the best guide to such perceptiveness is Marxism-Leninism-Mao Tse-tung thought, applied with a sound understanding of the principle of contradictions.[3]

Freud and his followers can be helpful at times in helping us understand the internal contradictions a person may be facing, but they do not provide an all-sided view. Similarly, many of the chic "radical" therapist crew have emphasized the environmental and social factors in peo-

[3]See Mao's *On Contradiction* (New York: China Books, 1967) and *On the Correct Handling of Contradictions among the People* (New York: China Books, 1966).

ple's distress. This is indeed a crucial component, but to emphasize it to the exclusion of the internal contradictions people face is also one-sided. (It, of course, follows that one reaction to the traditional focus on internal factors is to exaggerate the other side by focusing only on the external factors. The correct way to handle the situation is an all-sided appreciation of the component factors: understanding what is internal and what is external, and how the two interrelate.)

We need to encourage people's grasp of correct methods of thinking. We need to encourage the development of therapy centers, halfway houses, and the like, under the control of politically aware patient groups.

We need to help political groups and collectives understand the pressures that cadres face. Without falling into bourgeois psychology or self-cultivation, we need to help people grapple with problems of isolation, anxiety, depression, disappointment, and with the whole variety of problems that spring up around relationships with other people.

We don't think it's worthwhile today to encourage the elitist development of a new brand of specialist, the "radical therapist." We don't need another petty bourgeois elite to lead the revolution. We don't think it's correct for politically aware people to want to "be therapists." The goal is to do good revolutionary work, not find identity in bourgeois status.

We feel it's good to break down distinctions between therapist and patient. At the same time, we understand that some people are more helpful, more sensitive to others' problems, than other people. This usually has little to do with their level of "training" though.

People should join together to demand control of the institutions in their communities. Instead of focusing solely on alternatives—which tend to become utopian and (bourgeois) counterculture oriented—they could rally communities around the issues of controlling their own mental health facilities, programs for addicts and alcoholics, day-care centers, and so on.

The focus of all this needs to be maintained; helping one another is not an end in itself. The end is not self-cultivation or "growth." The end is revolutionary work: advancing the revolution which will transfer power in this society from the ruling class to the working class and its allies. In this context, helping one another becomes one of the tasks of helping the revolutionary cadre remain strong.

We don't feel radical therapists are needed to provide "radical therapy" to the masses of people and to revolutionaries. The people need a revolution, not therapy.

In terms of helping people through problems, we can encourage comrades to care for one another. When this is clearly too great a task, there are a variety of capable liberal shrinks who can help out, without laying their trip on the brother or sister needing help. (One of the cornerstones of liberal therapy is trying to maintain hands-off values.) The prime task of radical therapists is to become revolutionaries, not to deal with patients in the same old ways. Perhaps at some later stage we will need medics and therapists and other experts; right now we need the revolutionary cadre.

We don't encourage the groups of radical therapists who involve themselves in a variety of self-growth and encounter games and call it "revolution." Such activity is, at best, a compromise; at worst, a mockery of the struggle of the working and poor people of this country.

HOW PEOPLE CAN STRENGTHEN THEIR REVOLUTIONARY ASPECT WHILE REMAINING IN THE SYSTEM

Many therapists, and many people, feel they can't simply abandon their positions at the present time. For some, there are families to support; for others, an affluent life style to maintain. There may be "counterculture" jobs outside the system, at a reduced income, for some; for many, the choice is to remain a therapist or to be at a loss as to what to do for a living. Hopefully, many of these people will realize that as long as they are therapists, they are strengthening their bourgeois aspect, and will leave such jobs and take others. But understanding that people develop at their own pace and for many changing jobs is not now a possibility, we can discuss ways therapists might be able to strengthen the revolutionary aspects of their current jobs.

Any therapist who stays a therapist has to deal with the contradictions of that situation: bourgeois psychology and privilege versus a revolutionary "head." Our hope is that, understanding this situation, more and more young therapists will give up their privileged position and integrate with poor and working-class people. In the meantime, here are suggestions of things they might do:

As in this book, don't use "him" for the indefinite third person. Use "co" or "them." Shake up the sexism in our conventional language.

Bring your political views out into the open and talk to clients about what they mean.

Don't accept the usual standards of dress for being a therapist. Wear what makes you comfortable, and expose the class-by-dress ethic where you work.

Confront the reactionary professional notions in which therapy is steeped. Raise your hand, speak up, leaflet. Demand to have radical speakers where you work; demand nonprofessionals and patients as speakers, paid what other, "establishment" speakers get. Demand day-care facilities for parents attending meetings. Demand that all meetings be open to lower-echelon workers and members of the community served by the group meeting.

Talk to fellow workers about your perspective and your demands. Organize wherever you are.

Develop a power-structure analysis of your institution and destribute it. Help people understand the connections between their own power structure and that of the imperialist rulers of the country, the warmongers, the oppressors. Every hospital and mental health center in this country has someone on its board of directors who's making money from war, pollution, slums, and so forth. Expose them. Fight to get rid of them. Use that issue to educate people politically. Expose institutional sexism and racism, and the links of the institution to the capitalist system which profits from imperialism.

Demand power decentralization, community control of services, student control of education, worker control of the work setting, open admissions, and career-ladder programs that are open-ended at the top.

Radical staff *and* radical patients can write and distribute a radical newsletter. The newsletter staff should have an office and a phone extension where contact with newcomers and recruits can be made. Ask the boss or a board director for interviews. Expose the benevolent neutrality and "value-free" science of your local institution.

Look for potential allies among people organizing labor unions, among young students and alienated professionals, and in the community allegedly served.

Organize different levels of political entry. For example, "consciousness-raising" groups for men or women might be an easier point of entry than sitting in or picketing. Or start with a radical study caucus. Present a patient's case history emphasizing politically relevant points, concluding with a political analysis, not a psychoanalysis.

If you decide to have any meeting that has some political potential, advertise it heavily, making sure the boss knows about it. Hopefully, he (bosses are almost always "he") will respond. If a meeting room isn't available, demand and fight for one. Always try to draw lines separating you and your people from the boss.

Demand changes in services and expose their deficiencies. Fight to change teaching and research priorities to service priorities. In state hospitals and institutions of similar quality, try to influence staff and "patients"—an Insane Liberation Front, if you will. For example, at most state hospitals at least some patients lie in urine-soaked sheets all day. Complain to the administration, leaflet patients and staff, hold meetings in hallways and administrative offices, and even finally call in the media.

Demand innovative services—for example, home care, outreach, and preventive services. In order to see real alternative and innovative services, encourage people to visit Cuba, and to read about Chinese mental health care.

Fight involuntary commitment with a trial. Be part of a patients' rights movement. Expose failure to inform patients properly and legally (so-called informed consent). For example, most patients receiving research drugs or on research wards do not have a thorough understanding of what's going on or why they are in a research ward, rather than in a standard ward or even in the hospital. If patients are research subjects they should be informed and paid accordingly.

When you do "therapy," always suggest various political settings to help "patients" deal with their alienation and oppression. Always attempt to help patients understand the political causes of their "symptoms." Suggest to your patients that they work with existing political organizations, for example, women with women's liberation groups.

Support in any way all segments of the population particularly oppressed by psychiatry, namely blacks, Latins, women, homosexuals, youth, prison inmates, and anyone doing something politically relevant. Help raise bail for any political prisoner, especially if co is a member of the same oppressed group as you. At your next regular conference, rather than have somebody present a paper, do a guerrilla theater demonstrating what sexism is like in the "therapeutic" setting. If you're a therapy student and written tests are given, distribute your own counter-test, a test that asks real questions, especially about the institution you're at and about the institutions of psychiatry and psychology.

Encourage patients to talk to one another, to help themselves understand the *collective* nature of their symptoms. Encourage patients to engage in any of the above-mentioned actions or any other political actions, even if it is simply getting a group of patients to get together to discuss political issues.

Since even the most "private" hospitals and institutions have the major portion of their funds coming from public sources, demand that board of directors meetings be always open to the public. Demand that budgets and contracts be available for review. Work with community groups fighting for community control.

Embarrass and expose institutional failures by providing services it doesn't, but should, provide:

> 1. Lead poisoning is a major cause of mental illness and retardation in children living in metropolitan areas. Go to your local health department, get lead-screening kits, and go door to door in poorer neighborhoods. Any child with a positive test for lead should be brought to the hospital. Explain to each family why you're going door to door, talk about the politics of slum landlordism, and show how it is a direct cause of lead poisoning and mental illness.
>
> 2. Malnutrition is also a major cause of mental illness in poor children. Do a nutritional survey. Get a microhematocrit centrifuge to do iron deficiency

anemia studies as a screening test for malnutrition. Malnourished children should be sent to a Black Panther breakfast program or its equivalent. Mothers should be pushed to work with the local welfare rights organization. The politics of expensive ghetto groceries, the welfare system, and racism should be discussed more than psychiatric symptoms. Push welfare and/or Medicaid doctors to write prescriptions for food.

When institutional failings are noted, publicly expose them; literally petition for change. Petitions alone won't produce any results, but asking people to sign a petition at your centrally located petition table is a great way to start a politically relevant conversation. Use your professional prerogatives and privileges to infiltrate and educate.

Many people complain about the disruptive nature of many of these tactics, particularly in regard to conventions. The argument is advanced that disruption violates freedom of speech and press. It's our feeling that rights such as freedom of the press belong only to those who own one. The same applies to freedom of speech; if you don't have access to the media, all you can do is speak to yourself.

If you seize control of a convention meeting you can create your own meeting, open up a real dialogue, and have true freedom of speech. *Genuine and meaningful discussion cannot occur at a convention in America without first disrupting it.* Turn the convention into a political education meeting. The disruption is a protest against the elitism, racism, and sexism which abounds at any professional convention, simply by virtue of its being a "convention of professionals."

And what about those conventions and seminars which discuss the war and racism? Only a repressive form of tolerance would have a "debate" about or a "vote" on the war or racism. White Americans have no right to discuss the fate of Vietnamese or black people; they only need to get off their backs.

Here are some other reasons for the justified disruption of mental health conventions and seminars:

1. To protest the fact that conventions and seminars are a showpiece, a façade. They pretend that the mental health professions are open, responsive, and accountable. By definition, a profession is accountable only to itself and for that reason alone should be attacked.

2. To protest the repressive ideology of psychiatry and psychology which is both individualizing and alienating.

3. To produce a laboratory of reality that really deals with mental health and mental illness. For example, many people in the audience will be far more enraged about a disruption than they will be about the war. The fact that one can respond more strongly to disruption than to genocide is a measure of the crazed oppression of our society.

4. To delegitimize, demystify, and deprofessionalize mental health institutions. After all, anybody can take part in a disruption.

5. Last, and in some ways most important, is the role of exemplary action. With all our white-skin privileges, the least we can do is to be an example of white people in revolt.

It's true, it can be argued that it is better, more sensible, to stay inside the system and work patiently from within for needed reforms. This is the standard argument of people who have been subtly co-opted by having been given some autonomy and privilege within the system— so long as they do not upset the applecart. These people are the ones relied on to "cool out" dissent, to make liaison with the community, and so on.

The next step is to argue against not taking any overt action because it could jeopardize one's job. To say "Wait until I get that promotion, *then* I'll have the power to do what I want," is such sorry bullshit that it almost deserves no response. It is the same as saying all we have to do to change the capitalist system is elect McGovern instead of Nixon. It presupposes that people of good will, working within the system, will be able to change it significantly. What usually happens is that the good people get placed in positions where they are forced to act like pigs.

People will have to face the chance of being fired. Therapists should ask themselves every day why they are working for their institution anyway. They should ask themselves why they are therapists instead of in some more necessary revolutionary role. Then the nature of their clinging to their job will become clear.

Some people have responsibilities, have to support families, but people also have the capacity to change and build new ways of living when they see the necessity and urgency of doing so. The tendency for therapists is to do nothing rather than risk spontaneous action. They rest on their privilege and are "radical in their heads" but reactionary in their work.

This is, of course, precisely why the masses distrust professionals and therapists: they *know* which side the shrinks are on. They won't trust them until the shrinks stop shrinking for the system, until they confront their own class position and make attempts to change it. All other reformist work among therapists is liberal humanitarianism, needed of course, but far short of the maximum which people could contribute if they cut themselves free from class privilege.

10

Summary

WHAT THERAPY IS AND WHAT IT IS NOT

The critical question in evaluating psychotherapy is, "whose interests does it serve?" We have pointed out that psychotherapy in the United States has been created by a medical/professional elite, integrated into the mainstream of American capitalism and health imperialism, and has been used as an important tool of social control by the ruling class. Individual therapists have, at times, been helpful to their clients, in spite of the political superstructure surrounding therapy, but the primary tendency of therapy has been to oppress, not to liberate.

Thus, a person with a bourgeois world view, suffering from emotional problems, may find help with a traditional therapist from his own class background. Other classes cannot really expect much from therapy as it now stands. The radical-chic therapies—Gestalt, encounter, touchy-feely—appeal to an alienated and bored group of people; they have little to offer hard-working men and women whose emotional lives are chained and stifled by their condition. Utopian ideas have not made therapists more socially conscious. In fact, the opposite has been true. They have offered the individual therapist a safe escape from political reality.

The principal characteristic of therapy today is that it is bourgeois. The innovations and challenges of radical therapy groups—especially from nonprofessional and antiprofessional groups—is primarily revolutionary, and the stand of these groups deserves to be supported. The people who put out *Rough Times*, for instance, have elaborated an anti-imperialist revolutionary political line. They work with people involved in mental health issues, but not primarily with professionals. Rather, they focus on mental patients' liberation groups, prison groups, women's groups, the development of alternative centers for emotional support and help, sharing of skills and so on. Their work, primarily political, is not "therapeutic," of course, and they cannot provide a panacea for people who want a new "kind of therapy."

We feel focus on therapy alone will lead nowhere. We feel groups interested only in hospital reform, mental patients' rights, and so forth, have valid issues—guaranteeing bourgeois/democratic rights to people who are being denied them—but we feel they must go further if they are not to end up as "only reforms." This means constant political education, criticism/self-criticism, and challenge between these groups and those working in the working-class movement.

Therapists as therapists certainly have very few interests in common with working class, poor, and oppressed people. The therapy reforms they institute are likely to benefit only themselves. Those therapists who are genuinely interested in serving the people and advancing the revolution will have to abandon the position of privilege which insulates them from the masses.

So far, most efforts at founding a "radical therapy" have floundered on the internal contradiction between being a therapist and serving the revolution. Being a therapist of any sort fosters bourgeois characteristics (individualism, isolation from the masses, idealism, utopian thinking, lack of class consciousness) at the expense of revolutionary ones (the need to integrate with the masses, the abolition of caste distinctions, fees, mystified knowledge, the need for struggle and class warfare). Groovy therapists are using their radicalism to make money, write books (like this one), and claim the system's benefits. Calling it "ripping off the system" is nonsense; poor people and working people don't have this privilege and, in fact, are the people who are ripped off, not the publishers, or the TV stations. So long as therapists remain in the petty bourgeoisie and identify their interests with that class's, they cannot be fully revolutionary. To think otherwise demonstrates an incredible naïveté and lack of understanding. It is a counterrevolutionary position.

This is not to say that therapy skills cannot be useful to the revolution or in dealing with people. Of course they can. But the therapists who do such work *as therapists* are doing fundamentally liberal/humanistic work, not advancing the revolution. The revolution does not need its own therapists right now so much as it needs stalwart workers with an understanding of revolutionary—not petty bourgeois/professional—work. It's a matter of having to risk one's privileged position in order to do good work.

It's important to cut away the illusions people have about what value-free therapy actually is. It's important to cut away the mystery and magic about therapists being like mind readers, witch doctors, or faith healers. It's important to undermine the authority therapists have in this society, because they use it for serving the ruling class, not serving the people.

At the same time, it's important to maintain ways of being sensitive and helpful to one another, and to share what skills have been developed for dealing with various emotional problems. In revolutionary China, doctors and therapists are helpful. Industrial doctors or therapists *per se* are not bad; the problem is rather that they're used by those who control our society to oppress instead of help.

We must beware of anti-intellectualism in its antiknowledge, antiskill sense. We must learn to make our knowledge available to the people.

PSYCHOLOGY: RULING CLASS VERSUS REVOLUTIONARY OUTLOOK

Is it up to radical therapy to formulate yet another theory of psychology? We feel that endless abstract arguing over theory is not productive. Theory should develop from the summing up of experience, not from out of the sky. We're not interested in ways radical intellectuals can avoid class consciousness and struggle by debating.

Besides this, there already exists a good dialectical theory of psychology. Based on the principles of contradiction, it finds expression in Chinese psychiatry. According to this view, there are both extrinsic and intrinsic factors at work: that is, the society and social/political milieu provides one set of factors and predisposing factors within the patient, including inner conflicts, provide the other set. "External causes are the condition of change and internal causes are the basis of change, and . . . external causes become operative through internal causes."[1] Thus, in our society, external causes include the institutions of racism and sexism, the oppression of capitalism and of world imperialism. Internal causes include genetic factors, those patterns and conflicts in the society at large which have been "incorporated" into one's way of living. Thus, neurosis, psychosis, or "problems in living" can be understood as an interweaving of both factors. The theory of contradiction combines the intrapsychic/genetic orientation of the Freudians and psychiatrists with the notion that society itself is the principal determinant in

[1]Mao Tse-tung, *On Contradiction*, (New York: China Books, 1967).

many people's problems, an idea that has taken the brunt of the criticism of "radical therapy."

A one-sided approach to theory will be incomplete. An approach that only sees individual problems tends to be predominantly bourgeois, that is, serving the ruling class and bolstering ruling-class ideology. And that is, of course, how most therapy has been carried out in this society, and how most theory has evolved.

According to Ruth Sidel, the Chinese emphasize seven points in treating emotional problems: (1) collective help, (2) self-reliance, (3) physical therapy when needed (no electroshock), (4) heart-to-heart talks, (5) community ethos, (6) follow-up care, and (7) Mao Tse-tung's thought, "Arm the mind to fight disease," the practice of criticism and self-criticism, and the process of analyzing one's situation concretely. As she recounts the Chinese saying, "The socialist system is extremely beneficial to mental health because it eliminates objective contradictions between the individual and society." This would help explain the lower incidence of emotional problems in the People's Republic.[2]

We don't need any new "radical theory" of psychology. What we need is to sweep away the noxious notions of bourgeois psychology—the nonsense about penis envy, sex roles, and Freudian metaphysics; the ignorance of class conflict; the playing along with bourgeois institutions like the nuclear family, or strict heterosexuality. But bourgeois ideology can't simply be replaced by revolutionary thought in the textbooks; it involves a change in the entire structure of our society, and an actual transfer of power from one class to another.

In this sense, the main task is to involve ourselves more and more in the political struggles going on today. We

[2]Ruth Sidel, *Women and Child Care in China* (New York: Hill & Wang, 1973).

cannot separate "therapy" or "psychology" from the political context. We can't develop "radical therapy" apart from the revolutionary struggle, unless by radical therapy we're talking only about a safe, nonstruggle field of expertise.

We have to guard against the bourgeois aspects of the "cultural" revolution in our country—the notion, for example, that "it's happening all over, baby, so just lean back and it'll come." This attitude, that the revolution is "inevitable" and that people can just "do their thing" and see it arrive, is a betrayal of the class struggle. Only the affluent are going to swallow this line, not those who are suffering and oppressed day after day.

Of course bourgeois therapists will leap at the line that the revolution is coming, that people have to work "where they already are," and that building a "Marxist psychology" apart from the class struggle is their way of participating in it.

We have to combat this. Mental health centers and mental hospitals are *not* revolutionary bastions, and will not be so long as the solution is seen in terms of radical professionals leading change, or in terms of working within the system to defeat the system. The revolutionary aspect of mental health is the struggle of people against social/political repression. Wardens are not leaders of the struggle, no matter how friendly and open they are. No matter how groovy and right-on the therapists, psychotherapy is *not* creating a new cadre for the revolution. Therapy is a bourgeois institution in a bourgeois society: *That's* the reality. The revolution in mental health is to oppose the system and link mental health repression to other forms of pre-Fascist repression.

I learned this lesson from experience. When *The Radical Therapist* began in Minot, North Dakota, its founders were in the air force. The air force initially tried to intimidate us, but found that the journal was legal. From then on, the air force was quiet about *RT*. But when the same people began working in town—trying to organize airmen in an antiwar movement, starting a rap center for young people, helping women's liberation groups get started—the town bourgeoisie became infuriated. Actual involvement in the day-to-day life of people—rapping down the political line on drugs, speaking about sexism and chauvinism, linking individual problems to broader issues, speaking out about discrimination—brought down anger and repression. The town tried to get the founders of *RT* kicked out of the air force, or at least transferred. There was a big furor involving radio, church meetings, and so on. The point was this: Revolutionary work gets to the center of the people's struggle, and this threatens the ruling class. "Radical" intellectual ventures are tolerated because the people who own this country know that they present a lesser threat than action. It's a lesson we must learn from. Lead a strike in a factory, and repression comes down; write a radical article for petty bourgeois radicals, and nobody even cares.

THE MYTH THAT THERE ARE NO THERAPY SKILLS, OR THAT EVERYONE IS A THERAPIST

Sometimes correct ideas can be twisted into incorrect ones. Therapists today are a privileged elite whose training doesn't help them serve the people; rather, they learn to serve the bosses. Many people without formal training can really be "therapeutic" to people around them. Some people interpret this, however, to mean that everyone is a therapist, training or not, and that therapy "skill" does not exist. This attitude is idealist, detached from practical reality. It reflects a petty bourgeois attitude that the world really *is* the way we'd like it to be.

One result of this current fad is the frankly backward attitude that being a therapist is something worth our aspirations. It's become a middle-class, professionalist ambition. We've seen kids from the counterculture, with Laing in one hand and Perls in the other, asking to be (quickly, of course) trained as "radical therapists" so they can start treating clients. This is a reflection of impatient, petty bourgeois ambition. These people will even want to identify themselves as nonprofessional professionals. They have challenged the therapy establishment only to replace it with another.

To want to enter a privileged stratum of society is not a revolutionary attitude. The therapy freaks who see radical therapy in terms of personal advancement should be criticized.

It's different to push for sharing knowledge about human relationships with one's sisters and brothers. It's different to push for developing ways of caring for one another without reliance on the oppressive institutions of bourgeois therapy.

In a lengthy revolutionary struggle, we will all need to understand how to help one another, how to deal with severe emotional stresses. But this is different from being "therapists." It's one thing to develop self-sufficiency in a movement; it is another to attempt to carve a radical niche in the system as it is.

There is both a revolutionary and a reactionary element in the eagerness to deny therapy skill, and to proclaim that we're all therapists. So long as therapists are members of a professional elite, we shouldn't talk of *retaining* therapy but, instead, of "deprofessionalizing" it. That only means no longer pursuing therapy as it is practiced today. But the advocates of "everyone is a therapist" shrink in terror at the idea of losing their own privileges. They want "to organize where you already are." (Someone, apparently, has to organize the ruling class.)

This attitude reflects a fundamental ignorance of class struggle. Therapists and would-be therapists are, by their function, petty bourgeois. No matter how "radical" they are, they objectively serve the bosses. To bring about the revolution, therapy and other such institutions must be smashed, not "remolded from within" in a reformist way. They must be abandoned and destroyed. To try to hold on to the identity of therapist (or to develop ambitions in that direction) while at the same time laying claim to being revolutionary is misleading. Struggle and contradictions are facts which can't be wished away.

The goal should be to analyze what is known about therapy, take whatever is useful to the masses, and oppose therapy institutions as they currently exist. The slogan should be: "Therapists, put yourselves out of business!"

THE ILLUSION THAT THERAPY WILL CURE EVERYONE

People all over have been brutalized. Therapy has been advertised as a way of making people whole again. Either through "insight" or "letting your feelings out," or through some other (new) group or individual, body or mind treatment, people are supposed to get put together again. But the external causes of emotional problems won't change until the society changes. And the internal causes of emotional problems need to be acknowledged.

All the talk in the world about how society *should* be is irrelevant unless it begins with an understanding of where society *is*. We know that we have to deal with people who have been made emotional cripples. We can't expect them to throw away their crutches and walk just because we wish it so. Thus we have to deal with some people's need for a lot of care and therapy's incapacity to abolish the roots of mental suffering under capitalism.

What we want to underline in this book is that no new

therapy is going to provide the answer for unhappy people. The problem is political and so is the situation.

ADVICE TO PEOPLE WHO WANT THERAPY

We don't deny that many people are emotionally troubled. But we reject the idea that these troubles constitute an emotional "illness" that requires professional treatment. The "sickness" for us, is the capitalist/imperialist social and political system we all live under. The "treatment" for us is a good dose of revolution.

Of course we understand that many people need help in dealing with their feelings and problems. Often, people who are close political friends and comrades can help far more than any therapist. But sometimes, friends cannot deal effectively with a person's troubles, and someone else is needed. Often the person is needed because co can be objective and at the same time concerned, and can understand the subjective feelings of the person as well as the objective realities.

We have to face the fact that all of us have been crippled in some way by living in this society. The sexism which surrounds us, for example, affects each sexual relationship, and mingles power control and self-esteem with sex in unproductive and neurotic ways. The competition and subsequent feelings of helplessness, the alienation, these affect each of us deeply. We are exposed to constant psychic oppression, sex-role myths, media propaganda, distortions from the schools. External causes produce inner responses. As Fanon points out, we become people whose emotions are traumatized, people who are fearful, superdependent and depressed, people who cannot trust, people who are mixed up over assertion and aggression, over sex and lust. We have all been messed over and messed up.

For this reason, we understand that dealing with "individual solutions" is sometimes necessary. (And we know that what is necessary is correct.) We can raise collective awareness and support one another. There's no sense in being further drained and crippled.

After all, to speak about oppression in this society is one thing. To realize how it affects each of us is something else. Some people have indeed become casualties. We have all been brutalized, and none of us has escaped intact. We fear our own bodies, and are ashamed, guilty, and inhibited. We fear others and are supersensitive, suspicious, and hesitant. We are confused and lonely.

Some people, we must admit, need places to stay where they can be cared for while they pull themselves together. Others need medication to help them get a grip on their feelings. We do not think it does any good to shout "Courage!" at people and demand that they deal with the evil of the monster totally on their own. That some people are mistreated in hospitals does not mean that no one should be permitted to find a period of calm in some safe setting. That psychiatric drugs are overused does not mean that people who need to control unrelenting savage fears and terrifying feelings should not have access to medications which could help them out. In this, as in everything, we should avoid dogmatic thinking. We need to accept people where they are before trying to get them to move to where they could be.

Therefore, we understand that some people will need therapy help. The question is: How can they receive it in a decent unoppressive setting, under the people's control?

We feel that, often, people who suffer from emotional problems are looking for therapists to save them. Most therapy isn't going to meet their needs. We see the real solution to people's problems in collective, not individualistic, action; we see many problems as based in the external materialist conditions of bourgeois capitalist society. And these will not go away until the society changes. Many people's goals in therapy are really based on ruling-class ideology: to succeed at a piggish job or in an oppressive relationship, without altering the oppression; "to grow," with the focus on oneself. Therapy which tries to meet these goals is oppressive.

People who want to get into therapy ought to understand their goals, and whose interests these goals serve. We can't be enthusiastic about therapy which isolates people, makes them more competitive, reinforces their chauvinism, and maintains their positions in the ruling class or as servants to the ruling class. People who are forced to go into therapy or institutions by schools, courts, and so forth, need to be clear as to just whom the therapist is serving and how much to cooperate. Since therapy is not neutral in this society, people must know how much to cooperate with therapy ideas and programs.

We do feel people should turn first to their friends and co-workers for help. We feel therapists should be avoided unless there's no other alternative. We feel the principal means for getting one's problems together should be through collective political action rather than isolated therapy. All we can say to those who want to "get into therapy" is, "Watch out what you're getting into."

At the same time, we do understand that sometimes it's impossible to go on unless you get help with your emotional problems. And often a "third party" is what people must settle for, if a friend is not available or is not objective enough. Certainly when it's important to get together emotionally in order to go on with your life, you have to get help. What we're saying is that what's available often isn't adequate. It's like the mental hospital scene: Sometimes people really need to be away from the rest of the world, to sort out what they've been through, to unwind and then pull together. But for this need, in our country, most mental hospitals are grossly inadequate. The hospitals often make things worse with their rules, forced medication, psychological trips, and lack of civil rights for patients. Of course, you have to settle for the lesser evil when a problem comes up—it's important to be reasonable about things. But the ultimate goal isn't better, more available therapy; it's bringing about a revolutionary socialist country.

ADVICE TO PEOPLE WHO WANT TO BE THERAPISTS

People who want to be therapists ought to think about it again. Why join a professional elite that reinforces your most backward tendencies? We've had to struggle in recent years to defeat our own professionalism. Our professional training has been a drawback to genuine revolutionary work; only secondarily is it an asset to be used as we can. We wouldn't do it all over again. Basically, the medical/therapy trip has been a problem that has created profound contradictions within us both.

People whose view of therapists is that it's groovy to be one, like being a guru, or that it's a magical opening to self-knowledge or wisdom, are wrong. As it is now, therapy is a power trip, a way to succeed within the system. People who simply want to help one another can try to work at it on their own. Admittedly, there really isn't any training for nonprofessionals because therapy is a monopoly, and no outsiders are supposed to be let in. But people shouldn't fool themselves into thinking that they can find some training, stay "renegade," and still be therapists. Not if that's how they're going to make their living.

We are deeply wary of the ego trips and power trips of people who are therapists, and of those who want to be therapists. Because of that, we're not really sure what role "radical therapists" will ultimately have in revolutionary work. We've written about what people who can't change their lives now can do in the meantime—but that doesn't mean we're encouraging young radicals to become therapists.

WHAT IT COMES DOWN TO, IN A FEW WORDS

We're saying, don't get fooled by what therapy appears to be. If you want to get control of your own life, do it, but don't expect miracles from the bourgeois therapy scene—whether it's straight, groovy, radical, or whatever. You can get some help from therapy, but the real problem is political, and so is the solution.

Unite the many to defeat the few!
Therapists, put yourselves out of business!
Advance the new American revolution!

73 74 75 76 77 10 9 8 7 6 5 4 3 2 1